# The Problem of Employment Stabilization

# The Problem of
# Employment Stabilization

## BY BERTIL OHLIN

COLUMBIA UNIVERSITY PRESS · NEW YORK

# Preface

THE MAIN CONTENTS of this book is a series of Julius Beer
Foundation lectures I had the honor to give at Columbia University in the early part of 1947. Some material has been added
from the Chichele Lectures I had the honor to give at Oxford
University later in the same year, at the invitation of the
Warden and Fellows of All Souls College. I express to the
authorities and to my colleagues at these two great institutions
my sincere gratitude for invitations that enabled me to spend
two most stimulating and interesting periods in a scientific
milieu.

BERTIL OHLIN

*Stockholm,*
*February,* 1948

# Contents

# The Problem of Employment Stabilization

# 1. Aspects of the Economics of Over-full Employment

THE NORWEGIAN DRAMATIST IBSEN has made the statement that a truth usually lasts about twenty years. He was thinking chiefly about the rules of conduct in society. Sometimes one gets the impression that a scientific truth which has been widely accepted in the social sciences does not last even so long as twenty years. However, it would probably be more correct to say that the fashion changes are rapid and radical, at least in economic science. By this comparison I do not mean to imply that these changes are mainly arbitrary or artificial. As we change clothes with the climate, so economists vary their problems when new economic situations make them relevant and important. But in economic science we all seem inclined to overemphasize the things that differ from what we have been used to. Sometimes we tend to neglect the truths that have been established in the immediately preceding period.

In the 1930s the dominant problem for economic science was to analyze the causes of widespread unemployment and to find a cure for it. As unemployment, and a depressed economic state in general, was found to be due to insufficient demand for goods and services, the question became how to achieve and maintain a sufficient volume of aggregate demand. Some people think that this had so far been done only in times of war. Sir William Beveridge, for instance, has made the statement that war seems to be the only sovereign remedy for unemployment in modern liberal economic societies. While this no doubt is an exaggeration and was meant to be one, it contains an element of truth. The fact that employment conditions have almost always been good in periods of war but unsatisfactory during long periods of peace is a challenge to economists to outline a policy that would provide employment for everybody in occupations that are useful and desirable in peacetime. In dealing with this question, the emphasis has usually been placed on the difficulties that must be overcome in order to keep employment on a sufficiently high level. Beveridge sets the goal as follows: "Permanent full employment may be defined as a state of affairs in which there are always more vacant jobs than unemployed men." The Delegation on Economic Depression appointed by the League of Nations has stated that the primary objective of economic policy is to assure "that insofar as possible no man or woman able and willing to work should be unable to obtain employment for periods of time longer than is needed to transfer from one occupation to another or, when necessary, to acquire a new skill." It is only natural that the difficulties involved in maintaining a situation of such complete employment of labor has not as yet received as much attention as the difficulties in preventing a slump and in causing an expansion of employment from a depressed state. In the following pages I shall attempt to describe or characterize some of the difficulties which occur in a country that aims at maintaining conditions where everyone willing to work finds it easy to obtain a job. My object at this point is not to analyze the conditions of a relatively high degree of employment as experienced in good periods of business conditions between the two world wars. I assume a state of exceptionally complete employment in which the number of vacancies is as large as 4 or 5 percent of the total employment, and in which the unemployment due to movements of labor from one occupation to another is much lower than the number of vacancies. An analysis of a situation of this kind may throw some light on the important question of how to maintain a reasonably high and even employment. It may also help us to understand how high it is reasonable to fix the employment at which we should aim and which we therefore might, for practical purposes, call full employment. Let me, however, state at once that I intend to use the term full employment in this sense: Full employment is the degree of employment that exists when the aggregate demand for commodities is at the highest level that is compatible with the condition that demand at existing prices is balanced by current domestic supply.

It is possible that demand for commodities can exceed this level if an extra supply comes from abroad and is paid for by foreign credits or a reduction in the gold and foreign exchange reserves. It may also exceed it in a state where commodity stocks are falling, as well as where a portion of demand is left unsatisfied owing to "scarcities." Under such conditions employment may be more than "full." Full employment in this sense can exist when prices are rising, but hardly when they are falling. The percentage of the labor force that is employed in a state of full employment is relatively low (for example, 94 percent), in a country where great economic disturbances are taking place and where the mobility of labor is low. It is higher (for example, 97 percent) in countries with quiet economic conditions, a well-organized labor market and a skillful adaptation of public works to local surpluses of labor.

The state of affairs which I am to analyze can be called "over-full employment," or, for the sake of brevity, "over-employment." It is not, of course, incompatible with the existence of some structural and seasonal unemployment: it means simply that in most industries—not only in low-wage industries—there is a much greater number of vacancies than of people looking for jobs. The first thing we have to ask ourselves is how such a situation can be brought about. The answer is obvious. If the total demand for goods and services exceeds the current supply at present prices, producers will be anxious to expand output and will therefore increase their demand for labor. This is so even if practically the whole labor force is already employed. An expansion of output in an existing plant would appear unprofitable only if marginal costs were as high as prices of the goods produced in that plant. But in that case an expansion of the plant itself would be regarded as profitable, unless the great demand were looked upon as temporary; for prices must under these conditions be high relative to average costs. The problem therefore becomes the following one: what is it that will make the aggregate demand exceed the value at existing prices of the current supply of goods and services, which is forthcoming when practically all labor is employed? Does not demand depend on income and does not income depend on and vary with the volume of output?

It is true that income is dependent on production, though not entirely on the volume of goods that are put on the market in the present period, but rather on the volume of productive activity—in the widest sense of the term—that is now going on. And the demand for consumer goods depends on income and the willingness to save a part of it. But purchases for investment purposes are not financed exclusively by current income. A large part of investment is financed through credit, and the volume of new credit during a period has no fixed relation to the volume of present savings. Therefore, the sum total of what people are willing to buy for investment purposes and what they want to buy for consumption may well exceed or fall below the value of the forthcoming supply of goods and services at current prices. It is not necessary to complicate these matters by a detailed analysis of saving and investment of the kind that has become popular in the last decade. It is sufficient to point out that there is no automatic mechanism which guarantees that the sum total of what people want to buy for consumption and for investment will be exactly equal to the value of current output at present prices. If the aggregate demand is too large, relative to supply in a state of full employment, and if we grant consumers the right to determine how much they will buy, then one can say that what makes total demand too great is the fact that investment purchases are kept on an excessive level relative to the amount of income that people want to save in a state of full employment. In other words, *the state of overemployment is due to an excessive demand for investment purposes.*

Some cases of excessive investment are well known. This is true, for instance, of the ordinary inflation movement. Prices rise, wages go up, investment expands, prices rise still further in a cumulative process. Evidently if one wants to avoid a development of this kind as a result of an excessive investment demand, it is necessary to apply various governmental controls. This was tried in almost every belligerent country during the last war. Both wages and prices were kept down through official controls or semi-official agreements. The inevitable result was an acute feeling of scarcity both with regard to labor and commodities. Furthermore, when the total demand for products exceeds current output, the demand for labor increases. Sooner or later it will exceed the supply of labor at the current wage rates. This is the kind of situation I am going to comment upon. However, I shall not take the case of a war economy, because this involves too many special circumstances and too many specific psychological factors. It is probably more useful to analyze a state of affairs of overemployment as a semipermanent situation in peacetime. It is important to know what kind of state controls are required to make such a situation permanently possible. Above all we want to know *which economic advantages or disadvantages will follow from a system of this kind compared with one where a somewhat less complete employment is to be found.* These problems are, as a matter of fact, vital in many European countries.

Let us consider therefore a case that is common in Europe today. The prices of the most important goods and services are controlled. Wages, on the other hand, are not subject to government regulation. We are not concerned with the aftereffects of the war with regard to raw material supply and the scarcity of foreign exchange. With this important reservation we may have in mind the British economic situation before the outbreak of the foreign exchange crisis in the autumn of 1947. It has been stated that in Great Britain the annual volume of purchasing power available for consumption purposes in 1947 was about £7,000,000,000, whereas the current supply of the consumption goods and services was not much above £6,000,-000,000. I have some doubts as to the accuracy of such estimates. Let us assume a somewhat smaller discrepancy than this in order to make it possible to visualize a situation where there is no rationing of consumers' goods.

Let me try first to characterize the market situation under these conditions. As demand for many goods exceeds supply, most producers and traders find it easy to sell at current prices more than they have. From their point of view the situation is similar to what is called in economic theory "perfect competition." The marginal selling costs, that is, the costs required to sell one extra unit of the commodity at an unchanged price, are in such cases zero. This is so even if the number of competitors is small or if true monopoly reigns. In many firms, marginal costs of production are below prices which are equal to the marginal revenue. In other firms the marginal revenue curve slopes a little downward, but there is yet a difference between costs and revenue at the margin.

Every new laborer that can be employed therefore brings a considerable extra profit. Firms in this situation continue to advertise largely in order to hold the market *in the future,* when conditions have changed. In these conditions the demand for labor must exceed the supply. Let us look now at what happens on the commodity markets. It is inevitable that commodity stocks should be reduced unless speculative considerations make the owners of these stocks refuse to sell. In the case of domestic raw materials and half-finished products, bottlenecks develop, for there are always some lines of production in which capacity is relatively smaller than in other lines. Buyers of certain goods like machinery that is made to order are put on waiting lists. Thus, in spite of the use of overtime, which to some extent alleviates the pressure, it is obvious that the investment in new productive appliances, houses, and so on, is delayed. The total volume of investment will be smaller than planned and anticipated. Some of the consumers' purchases are also delayed because the desired type of goods is not to be found immediately. In other words, "unintentional" savings, caused by the putting off of purchases, appear. In some industries profits may become unexpectedly large, and in that way, too, unintentional savings are created. Thus, the volume of investment is made to agree with the volume of savings although much more investment was planned than would correspond to the planned savings. It is possible that part of the investment is financed by the drawing upon foreign exchange reserves. For the excessive demand will tend to make the volume and value of imports rise, whereas exports fall off. To the extent that the price control is incomplete or ineffective, prices will go up. This may increase profit and savings and reduce the volume of goods that are consumed.

Considerations of this kind lead us to an important conclusion. *It is impossible to have a situation of overemployment without getting bottlenecks in the domestic economy.* There are not sufficient goods to be had and the degree of insufficiency will be very uneven. As it is necessary to expand the capacity in certain lines, before output can be increased, the shortage in supply of these goods may be intense. In other fields supply can be more easily adjusted. The conditions on the labor market about which I shall speak below will, however, make adjustments in production more difficult than what we are used to under conditions of less complete employment. In countries which have scanty reserves of foreign exchange, bottlenecks will appear for another reason, that is, an insufficient supply of imported raw materials and other goods. If large buffer stocks exist at the time when the period of over-investment begins, then the appearance of bottlenecks may be delayed. But sooner or later shortages will develop. If certain prices are not regulated they will tend to rise considerably, particularly in the case of raw materials. For it is better for producers to pay a high price than to curtail production. It is not unlikely that the most serious bottlenecks will appear with regard to some half-finished products for which capacity is insufficient. Supply of such goods is often inelastic, as the building of new plants may require several years. If many countries gravitate into a state of overemployment the effect on raw material prices on the world market will be unavoidable. It is difficult to see how a considerable but uneven rise in such prices can be avoided. As the pressure grows, it will be increasingly difficult to maintain a control of prices without rationing. Besides, the volume of investment will tend to grow, and if the situation is not to run entirely out of hand it will be necessary to control investment activity.

Let me add that the shortage of labor cannot be abolished through immigration. Let us assume that there are in a country 100,000 vacancies and that, therefore, the same number of immigrants are admitted into the country. These newcomers appear not only as workers but as consumers as well. Thus, demand will grow and supply will continue to be insufficient. It is true that the total volume of savings will grow, as a part of the increased output and income will be saved, but investment will have a tendency to rise also, as the need for housing will increase.

If we compare the situation I have now briefly outlined with conditions at a moderate but relatively high level of employment, we find that there are several advantages connected with the former. First, the very full employment is in itself an indication that production is relatively large. Secondly, the scarcity of labor acts as a stimulus to rationalization. Investments that increase output with a constant labor force are given preference both by businessmen and by the government agencies that have a say on investment policy. Furthermore, trade unions will probably be less adverse to labor-saving devices than they have usually been hitherto and may even be strongly interested in methods that increase efficiency and earnings. Thirdly, selling costs will be much lower than under ordinary economic conditions. This may be a saving of the order of magnitude of, perhaps, 1 percent of the national income, probably less. Fourthly, the feeling among workers of all kinds that there is little risk of unemployment, for the time being at least, and that it would be easy to find a new job must be counted as a considerable gain.

On the other hand, one cannot overlook that there are in the state of overemployment several offsetting influences which tend to reduce the effectiveness of the economic system. I have already mentioned that bottlenecks and waiting lists for deliveries of machinery, half-finished products, and some raw materials will be inevitable. This means that production will be slowed down, perhaps in a whole industry, as a result of a temporary lack of vital commodities. It will prove impossible to maintain a continuous process of output. The Swedish experience in 1947 brings out that the losses caused in this way are considerable. In the building industry an expansion of the labor force by about 10 percent above the 1946 level seems to have brought practically no increase in total output. This, no doubt, was due also to an increase in the irregular absence from work. In 1948 it caused a loss of 2 percent of the total number of man hours in manufacturing industries, over and above the loss of a similar type in pre-war years.

Another unfavorable factor is the excessive labor turnover that seems to be characteristic of a state of overemployment. Even in Russia where conditions are different from the capitalistic economies, there is a complaint that capricious movements of workers from one job to another reduce efficiency. The experience in Sweden in recent years bears out that such arbitrary migration back and forth not only reduces the output of the workers in question but to some extent hampers the work of other laborers who are dependent on the former. According to a Swedish investigation for the mechanical industry in the years 1918–46 labor turnover has with a surprising regularity varied in reverse proportion to the volume of unemployment. In 1945 and 1946, when unemployment had already reached a minimum, labor turnover rose rapidly, as the state of overemployment was intensified. See chart on p. 14.

It is perhaps somewhat of a paradox that labor mobility of another type tends to be relatively low where overemployment rules. In the past, unemployment in some occupations has been an important stimulus to transfers to other places and occupations. During a period of overemployment, there will be very little of such unemployment and many firms will tend to hold their workers even if they are not needed at the time, fearing that once they are dismissed it may be impossible to get them back again. Furthermore, the psychological obstacles to movements from one place to another will be great in the case of stable, conservative workers. Besides, if rents are controlled and are not allowed to rise to a market equilibrium level—and this is for obvious reasons almost never the case in

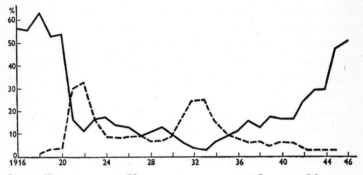

LABOR TURNOVER AND UNEMPLOYMENT IN THE SWEDISH MACHINE-TOOL INDUSTRY

Percentage of workers who have voluntarily left employment during each year —————
Unemployment percentage  – – – – –

a period of overemployment, otherwise rents would go to excessive heights—one has to reckon with a shortage of housing. Hence, industries located in areas where the housing shortage is acute will find it particularly difficult to attract new labor. As a result there arises a tendency for business firms to establish new factories in districts where the labor supply is relatively satisfactory, even though a given district may offer less favorable conditions with regard to cost of transport or in other respects. Hence the location of new industries will not be the most effective one. Evidently, the expansion of output in industries producing goods that are needed in larger quantities may be difficult in the face of such low mobility of labor.

In some countries, like Great Britain, one has tried to remedy this unwillingness of the labor force to accept employment where it is most needed. Tentatively, various methods of directing labor to such occupations and to check migration from them are being tried out. It is not surprising that a policy of direction and control of industry has a tendency to spread to the labor market. For output cannot be increased without access to labor power.

Of course, firms and industries which happen to have an unused productive capacity can expand their output more easily than others which are dependent on the building of new factories. There is no a priori likelihood that the former are always those which can add most to the national product. On the contrary, it seems probable that the expansion of output when compared with demand will be somewhat unbalanced.

Experience in Sweden and other countries seems to indicate that while large firms experience difficulty in finding the needed labor force, small firms can expand because they are in a position more or less secretly to pay wages above the level fixed in the collective agreements. In some cases the efficiency of production is lower in the small firms but even for them the marginal revenue may well exceed the marginal cost in a state of overemployment. It is also obvious that it will be very difficult for an industry to expand unless it is a high-wage industry, particularly in countries where the number of people in the working age is not increasing. For instance, if more textile goods are needed, and I think this is the case in many countries today, the textile industry nevertheless finds it very

difficult to expand its output because its wage-rates are relatively low. It may even lose labor to other industries in spite
of the unsatisfied demand for its products. This has been the
case in Sweden in recent years. To transfer an important industry, at once, from a relatively low-wage status to a high-wage
status is, of course, extremely difficult. If it were tried, it would
have far-reaching consequences on the whole wage level as
well as on the price structure. Obviously, there are several
reasons why one must expect a relatively slow adaptation of
supply to demand for different goods. It can be done much
more quickly whenever there is not such an excessive scarcity
of labor. It is a sad conclusion that the smooth adaptability
of the economic system to some extent depends on the existence of a certain amount of unemployment. However, it is
important to stress that the disadvantages mentioned above
seem to a large extent to depend upon the change from the
stage of full employment, where they are much less intense, to
one of over-full employment. What I have said is by no means
an argument for a low level of employment.

The control of prices which is inevitable under conditions
of overemployment will, in countries that are reluctant to an
expansion of the bureaucratic apparatus, be confined to the
more important commodities. This may lead to an ineffective
use of the productive resources. It is natural that the control
should be directed primarily towards goods and services that
are important for the consumption of the general public and
particularly those which enter largely into the costs of living
indices. Hence, the pressure to keep prices low will be stronger
in the case of such products, and producers will find it tempting to expand the output of other, less severely controlled and

less important, commodities. During the price control in the United States it was found to be easier to buy fancy shirts at $8 to $10 than standard shirts at $3 to $4. New investment to expand capacity will be similarly directed into channels that are not advantageous from the point of view of society as a whole, that is, channels that do not supply the goods which are in the most intense demand. Small factories are built and put into operation by new firms, even though the capacity of existing factories with greater efficiency cannot be fully utilized.

I mentioned above that a certain reduction in selling costs is possible when the demand for most goods exceeds supply. This saving will, however, be more or less offset by *the increased difficulties involved in buying* the right kind of goods. We must remember that commodity stocks in some lines will be relatively low, the more so the longer the state of overemployment lasts. Hence, consumers will often have to wait in queues and to go from one shop to another to find what they need. Similarly, professional buyers must spend a considerable amount of time in finding the right sources of supply and to persuade producers to put out the wanted products. They tend to keep in stock large quantities of these scarce commodities that they have been able to buy, perhaps for a future need. An unbalanced composition of stocks of materials of this sort tends to slow up production—as already mentioned—for one producer has managed to store one type of goods and another producer other types, while each has to wait for what he is missing. Present conditions (1947) in Europe offer ample illustration of this phenomenon.

Scarcity of labor will also lead to the establishing of waiting lists for people who want repairs done by carpenters, plumbers, and so on. Some years ago I read a story of a Russian lady who was trying to persuade a plumber to repair a leakage in the bathroom without having to wait three weeks for the job to be done. The humble attitude of the lady and the superior attitude of the plumber did not remind one of a state of absolute equality in society. The plumber rather made one think of an upper-class person in the old Russia, who might or might not heed the supplication from another person in a very dependent position. People in other countries seem to have had similar experiences. Anyhow, the necessity to wait for weeks before repairs can be done is a disadvantage worth mentioning.

Another cause of waste connected with a state of over-employment is the increase in the number of people required for the administration of rationing and regulation and in the greater amount of clerical work that is spent in the handling of such questions in the business firms. To a large extent, at least, this labor force is withdrawn from "productive" employment.

It is, of course, impossible to say whether the economic advantages that follow when we proceed from a state of full employment to a state of overemployment, above all the more complete utilization of labor, will offset or more than offset the various disadvantages I have touched upon, even if we should accept such a crude standard of measure as the quantity of output. The only thing one can say is that it is very doubtful whether an increase of average employment from, for instance, 96 percent to 98 percent—apart from seasonal unemployment—will add to the volume of output. The loss in efficiency may more than offset the increase in the number of hours worked and irregular absence from work may keep this increase much below the 2 percent. Personally, I am inclined to think that output would in the long run be maximized at a level of employment high enough to create a feeling that it is uncertain whether the labor force can be increased in a firm or not—such a feeling is a stimulus to rationalization—but not so high that it would be called over-full employment with the terminology I have used above. However, it is quite possible that production will be the highest if employment varies with some regularity between a little below and a little above full employment.

A simple illustration of the probable relation between total output and employment in a country has been worked out by a Swedish economist, Professor Svennilsson:

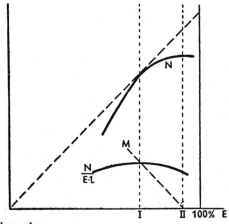

N=National product

E=Employment percentage

$\dfrac{N}{E \cdot 1}$=Output per man hour (1 is the constant number of working hours "available")

The production function $N = f(E)$ reaches its maximum when employment E is in position II. If output per man hour were constant ( $= h$), then we would have $N = h \cdot E$. The output per man hour reaches maximum when employment E is in position I. The marginal productivity of labor follows the line M and is zero in position II. It seems quite likely that conditions in Sweden in 1947 corresponded to this picture. However, the possibility of an increased use of overtime has to be considered.

Let me turn now to another aspect of the economic system that is characterized by over-full employment. *Is it probable that a relatively stable price level can be maintained* in the long run? If the answer is in the negative, and if we find—as I think we shall—that a considerable rise in price levels is probable in the long run, then this must in itself be regarded as a weakness of such a system. For such price movements call forth changes in the distribution of income which are generally regarded as undesirable. Furthermore, strong price movements not only make it difficult to maintain a balanced economy but also increase the risk that some day a violent recession will set in. This would, of course, involve a great loss and we are entitled to put the risk of it as an item on the debit side of the system of overemployment.

I have already mentioned that there will be a tendency for employers to "overbid," to pay higher wages than are agreed upon in collective agreements. In Sweden the rise in the weekly earnings of industrial workers in 1946 is estimated to have been 8 percent, of which one half is supposed to be due to such "overpayment," for example in connection with the fixing of piece rates that are not determined in the collective agreement.

When new wage agreements are negotiated in a state of over-employment the unions will be likely to ask for considerable wage increases. For decades they have asked for large increases when business was good and to accept constant or even reduced wage rates when business was bad. It is, therefore, improbable, except in very special circumstances, that—in a period of an extraordinary scarcity of labor—they would be content to accept increases of the magnitude of 2–3 percent, which corresponds to the "normal" increase in productiveness during a year. The claim for higher wages will be strengthened, if profits are high, and this has so far been the rule in most countries since the war. To the extent that profit margins cannot be reduced, increased wages will bring a pressure on prices to rise. Unless investment purchases are reduced when wage payments rise faster than productivity—which tends to reduce profits and corporation savings—aggregate purchases will grow and tend to lift prices, even if profit margins are large. The effectiveness of price control to prevent this is limited. The experience of the United States, Sweden, and many other countries in 1946 and 1947 bears this out. The employers' resistance to large wage increases will probably be relatively weak when labor is very scarce. Low wage industries, in particular, may be willing, perhaps anxious, to raise wages in order to keep or expand their labor force. The existence of price control will, of course, tend to reduce this willingness to lift wages. But the fact that marginal revenue is for most firms higher than marginal costs will nevertheless lead to wage increases.[1] Under such conditions it will prove impossible to maintain a ceiling on all important prices in the long run. When the

[1] See the argument in Appendix I.

ceiling is broken in one way or another, prices may rise considerably; if it is maintained for a long period and if employers, therefore, refuse to grant wage increases acceptable to the trade unions, the outcome may be large labor conflicts. It cannot, I think, be denied that, when a typical seller's market reigns on the labor market, the risk of either considerable price movements or large conflicts is much greater than it would otherwise be. This is a serious weakness of the system of maintaining over-full employment. Besides, if people should come to expect a long-run tendency of rising prices, this may have consequences for the lines of investment chosen as well as for the willingness to save; in both cases the consequences will by commonly accepted standards be regarded as not advantageous.

In a state of overemployment and insufficient capacity there will be—as experience demonstrates—a tendency in many industries to increase capacity. Hence, *the volume of desired investment will tend to grow.* If it is to be kept at a level compatible with moderate overemployment, then either the interest level has to be raised, credit restrictions applied, or investment directly regulated. It is quite probable that when the state of overemployment and excessive demand has lasted for some time, the tendency to increase investment will be so strong that, if credit and investment restrictions are not to be used, the interest level has to be raised to a considerably higher level than under ordinary conditions. Obviously, an economic situation of this sort is inherently very unstable. If for one reason or another the volume of investment is suddenly reduced or a consumers' strike begins and, therefore, the total demand for goods and services declines, a strong tendency to a recession may set in. This will call for a drastic reduction in interest rates and other measures, but it is not at all certain that a temporary recession can be avoided.

Many European countries have preferred to use investment control rather than high interest levels that would exercise a disturbing and unpredictable influence on house building and on rents in new houses. It is not surprising that the pressure of the excessive demand, which is the characterization of over-employment, leads to an economic policy of this sort.

A special difficulty with a policy of maintaining a state of overemployment is that it tends to cause *a drain on the reserves of gold and foreign exchange* for the country in question. How strong that drain will be depends, *inter alia,* on business conditions in other countries. If one country has a higher degree of employment than the rest of the world, its balance of payments tends to be weak. Only temporarily will it be possible to offset this tendency by maintaining a relatively low value of the national currency. Then, as such a valuation will tend to raise prices and as price levels under these circumstances will have a rising tendency anyhow, a policy of continued depreciation will probably be called for. To avoid this, the institution of exchange control can, of course, be used. Only the United States would be in a position to maintain overemployment for a long time and to lose gold without any serious weakening of her international liquidity position. Of course, overemployment might be possible in other countries, too, if foreign capital flowed in on a sufficiently large scale. Thus, a state of relatively free international trade, when some countries maintain a state of overemployment, assumes a free and easy movement of capital and a willingness on the part of the capitalists to invest large sums of capital abroad without asking for great differentials in return on the capital. If this condition is not fulfilled (and this is most unlikely to be the case for many years to come) restrictions on trade—direct import regulation or foreign exchange restrictions—will be caused by the overemployment. Small countries in particular must expect that an increase in total demand by a few percent above a full-employment level will exercise a very considerable pressure on their foreign exchange position. This is what Sweden has experienced since 1946.

The fact that *overemployment is, as a matter of fact, incompatible with relatively free international trade* is an interesting parallel to the well-known observation that depressions foster restrictive trade practices, although usually for quite different reasons.

If and when the gold and foreign exchange reserves become exhausted or reduced to a minimum, a country dependent on the importation of foreign raw materials may find it difficult to maintain an even and adequate supply thereof. The outcome is likely to be a decline in productivity and temporary unemployment. In a situation of this sort the importation of foreign machinery will probably be much reduced over certain periods, with a slowing down of rationalization of industry as a consequence. Furthermore, countries that have come into an illiquid international position often find that they cannot arrange their international trade on so favorable terms as before. Bilateral trade practices will be used and, hence, it will not always be possible to purchase in the cheapest markets. It is probable that the insistent domestic demand for a country's own export goods will keep exports on a low level, thus necessitating severe import restrictions. In this way, even such foreign goods may be excluded that have a much greater usefulness than the "marginal" quantities of the export goods that are being consumed at home but which would, in a more balanced employment situation, be exported in exchange for the vital imports. All these things are examples of waste and reduced effectiveness that follow from an attempt to maintain a state of overemployment.

From considerations of this sort—based largely on the experience of European countries in the last two years but independent of the aftereffects of the war—the general impression is that a state of over-full employment cannot last for a considerable period unless a system of rather strict government regulation is used. Furthermore, it seems highly doubtful whether the volume of output will be increased when employment passes from full to over-full employment. By full employment I mean, as already mentioned, the state in which the aggregate demand for goods is the highest that is compatible with the condition that it should be balanced by current supply at existing prices.[2] The idea of keeping the "volume of purchasing power" permanently well above the "equilibrium level" in order to guarantee to everybody an easy access to employment is evidently not such a brilliant one as many people came to think during the last war. On the contrary, I am inclined to maintain that it is wise to let economic policy aim

[2]It is a special problem—not to be discussed in this connection—to what extent an economic policy that leads to overemployment is reasonable as a temporary measure during the period of reconstruction after the war in order to compel the people to keep down their consumption and, thus, make a relatively large investment possible. Such a policy is then an alternative to a policy of budget surpluses and more severe rationing. In Norway a consideration of this sort has been given much weight by some influential politicians.

at the just-mentioned appropriate level of total demand and employment where general scarcity plays its customary role as a balancing and economizing force, even if such a policy should, as a matter of fact, lead to an average employment below this standard, as some cyclical variation will be impossible to avoid. The alternative seems to be a system of more and more controls and, unless they are tightened to include wage policy as well, finally considerable inflation. Thus, to keep up total demand at a level where it is very easy for anyone to find a job is no panacea for our economic ills. It is better to set a different goal: to create and maintain a balanced economy, where total demand is large enough to provide employment practically the whole time for practically all labor that is available in the appropriate places and occupations, but where there is no considerable number of vacancies in industries paying normal wages. To achieve this will indeed be difficult enough.

# 2. Investment Policy and Employment Stabilization

I SHALL NOT ATTEMPT to compete with the writers who have recently published books on employment policy that discuss long lists of the various measures relevant to an analysis of national policy to maintain a high and even volume of employment. I shall try, rather, to comment upon certain important fundamental relations that have a bearing on this problem. Some illustration of appropriate methods is found in Chapter 4.

Obviously, the volume of employment depends on the volume of current output, measured as "value added by manufacture" relative to the height of the wage or earnings level, with due regard to the shares of the net national income that are paid out as rent, interest, and profit. Furthermore, changes in the volume of output are due to changes in the volume of aggregate expenditure. In an analysis of employment one cannot discuss the changes in the volume of aggregate expenditure without considering that it must be measured in terms of the average wages or earnings of one unit of labor, or—if expressed in money—must be compared with changes in the average level of wages. It is important to keep this fact in mind. Possible variations in the distribution of income, i.e., a change in the relation between the income of labor and other types of income, have to be considered, also. The share of profit changes considerably with the business cycle. Hence, employment does not vary in precise proportion to aggregate expenditure, even if the level of earnings is constant.

The different kinds of expenditure can conveniently be classed in five groups—a practice that has become usual in the last years: 1) purchases for private consumption; 2) public expenditure on current account; 3) private investment; 4) public investment; 5) net foreign investment.

It is generally accepted that stability in employment to a very large extent depends on stability in investment,[1] and that therefore the sum of private and public investment at home and net foreign investment is the "strategic" quantity. If people and institutions want to save a certain proportion of the national income compatible with full employment, then full employment is possible only if the volume of investment is appropriate to this willingness to save. The other part of the output will be purchased for consumption purposes. The willingness to save is not an expression of an individual propensity only; it depends also on the methods used in the life insurance industry, the business policy of corporations, and surpluses or deficits in the public finances. It is doubtful if one can conveniently group these things together under a common propensity-to-consume function for society as a whole.

If the willingness to save should vary, an adaptation of the volume of investment will be necessary, unless the willingness to save has changed as a result of deliberate policy by public bodies so as to bring about an adaptation of savings to a certain changed volume of investment activity. However, as a first ap-

---

[1] This is not an idea that was brought to the fore by Keynes' General Theory, as writers of the "Keynesian school" have asserted. It has been stressed in many writings in business cycle theory in the 1920s and earlier, e.g., in articles on "the acceleration principle." It more or less dominates all Swedish books on employment policies published in the years 1930–35. The present chapter follows the lines of my paper on "Investment Stabilization and Price Stabilization" (in *Essays in Honor of Irving Fisher*).

proximation, I think one can say that if we want to stabilize the aggregate expenditure and the volume of employment, we must aim at *keeping the volume of investment on a relatively stable level*.

Let me begin with *private* investment. There are two kinds of private investment: the professional investment by business people and the investment by consumers, who buy durable consumer goods. Dwellings may be classified under the one or the other, but I prefer to place them in the former category. Private *professional* investment depends largely on profit expectations, although not in a way that can be described in a simple formula. Hence, it is desirable that costs and sales prices should not get out of line with each other. Nor must expectations as to the quantities that one can sell be subject to violent fluctuations, if we are to get the desired stability. Of course, in individual cases—with regard to certain commodities or a certain industry—this happens all the time; but for the economy as a whole, economic stability requires that the cost and price relationship and development be such that, on the whole, profit expectations do not become much more pessimistic or optimistic than they are in a stable situation where the volume of employment is at the desired level.

## WAGE-PRICE RELATIONSHIP

The relation between costs and sales prices is particularly important in industries where real investment—production of capital goods—is large, for instance in the housebuilding industry. The most important item in costs is wage payment per unit. Taking the economy as a whole, this is obvious. Hence, the relation of wage rates per unit of output to the price per unit of output in the investment industries is highly important. If wage rates are determined by bargaining and the efficiency of production cannot be rapidly increased, it is important that prices can adapt themselves to these conditions of cost. To have free wage movements and controlled prices is in the long run not compatible with full employment, unless such an adaptation is permitted by the controlling agencies.

Profits depend also on the volume of business. For this reason, it is not only necessary that prices should bear some normal relationship to cost; it is also necessary that the prices of investment goods should bear some balanced relationship to the purchasing power of the people who are either to buy these investment goods or to buy the consumers' goods which they help to produce. In the case of dwellings and many other things, it is the average income level of the consumers that is the source of the demand. So prices of investment goods must bear some reasonable relation to the average income level in society as a whole.

If the costs of new houses and their prices go up, relative to the average income level, it is natural to expect a fall in the demand for new houses and a decline in investment. Hence, it is highly important—I personally think that, if any one relation can be singled out, this is perhaps the most important of all—that *costs in the building industry do not get out of line with the general income level.* Monopolistic price and wage policies in investment industries like house-building may raise costs and prices and, thus, reduce the volume of investment in such a way as to curtail the total volume of employment.

Some economists stress the fact that the volume of investment depends on the development of consumption. We all know about the "acceleration principle": new investment depends on the *rate of change* in consumption; therefore, some people say it is the rate of change in consumers' income that is really the strategic factor. I agree, of course, that investment in house-building, the manufacturing industries, and, to some extent, everywhere, is influenced by the rate of change of consumers' incomes. But it seems to me to be almost inconceivable that the development of consumers' income should vary up and down in the very specific manner necessary to call forth automatically a relatively stable volume of investment! Hence, the rate of change of consumption is not a factor that can be manipulated to make the whole system relatively stable.

## IMPORTANCE OF CONSTRUCTION AND PUBLIC INVESTMENT

The new investment in factories and machines for the consumers' industries is certainly less than half the total volume of investment in countries like the Western democracies. The investment in house-building, in public utilities, and in the construction and expansion of cities seems to be in most cases by far the largest item, and in some cases constitutes more than 50 percent of the total. So if the volume of investment handled by, say, the municipalities in public buildings, in new streets, and in new city communications, and so on, plus the volume of investment in housing (which is more or less under public control in different ways in many countries) could be kept on a relatively stable level, then it would form a nucleus of stability in the economic system. Once this is done, it would not be very difficult to keep within reasonable limits the inevitable variations in some other investment lines, as factory industries, and to offset them by changes in those that are under direct public control. It goes without saying that the price-cost relationship in consumers' industries has an influence on the former type of investment.

So far, when analyzing costs, I have mentioned only labor costs. But *interest rates* are, of course, also an important cost item, not in consumer goods industries, but in the investment trades, including housing. Therefore there is, a priori, an argument in favor of varying the interest level if we want to affect the volume of investment through a change in the cost-price relation in investment industries and through a change in the relation between prices of investment goods and the general income level.[2] On the other hand, there is a strong argument against it in countries with a large government debt. Changes in the interest level cause fluctuations in the capital values of long-term bonds and other things too, and this may affect the financial strength of the banking system and the insurance companies. A considerable rise in the interest level might reduce the value of bonds so much as to endanger the position of some banks that are otherwise quite stable. In some countries, where the banks own large quantities of bonds, it is therefore an important problem whether it is possible to construct a system permitting variations of the market long-term rate of interest for new loans and at the same time limiting the repercussions on the banks of these fluctuations in interest rates and in capital values. If that could be done, then it would be easier to use changes in the interest level as a means of affecting the volume of investment.

Interest policy might then perhaps come into its own again

[2] It goes without saying that a system of licensing building activity can be used, instead, to affect the volume of investment. The relative advantages and disadvantages of these two methods I cannot discuss here.

at least in economic theory—after having almost disappeared
for ten years, as evidenced by the fact that many economists
have talked about a permanent tendency to oversaving and
underinvestment, without mentioning the possibility that a
lower long-term rate of interest than the one that existed in the
thirties could increase investment and reduce savings.

### INVENTORY FLUCTUATIONS

A special sort of professional investment consists of *commodity stocks*. They may vary suddenly. As a matter of fact,
they often do, because if consumer demand falls off, retailers
are apt to reduce their stocks. Therefore, the retailers' demand
from producers or wholesalers will fluctuate more violently
than the consumers' demand.

I am leaning to the view—a very tentative one—that one
important reason why a small recession often develops into a
more serious one is this reaction by professional buyers and their
tendency to reduce inventories when their own sales go down.
Therefore, one important aspect of any anti-depression policy
would seem to be to reduce the capricious changes in inventories. Measures to achieve this have not been much discussed.
However, it is obvious that if the commodity price level is kept
relatively stable, there is less inducement for retailers to vary
their stocks. The risk of fluctuations in *individual* commodity
prices would not be an incentive for retailers to vary their
stocks so much as they have been doing in the last decades.

### CENTRAL BANKING CONTROLS, WAGES AND PRICES

In my opinion the development of the commodity price level
in the next decade or two will depend chiefly on the develop-

ment of wage rates relative to efficiency. Central banks will have small chance of influencing the commodity price level, except in so far as they can use credit policies to prevent a state of overinvestment and overemployment and, thereby, affect wage policy. What made central banks so powerful before 1914 was the fact that they had the power to create depressions. If prices tended to rise the central banks could restrict credit and raise interest levels, reduce investment, and cause unemployment; in this way, they could even in exceptional cases bring about some wage reductions. At least they could prevent further wage increases for a certain period, a couple of years or so. But if economic policy in general will aim at the maintenance of a high and even level of employment, the banking system will lose not only its power to create depressions but also much of its influence on the trend of wages and prices. Therefore, if we want to maintain relatively stable commodity price levels— and that is certainly helpful in any policy of employment stabilization—it would seem necessary to obtain in some other way a reasonably stable wage level, or rather a wage level that rises at about the same rate as productivity.

When a depression has started it is, as a rule, not useful to reduce wage rates except those that are out of line with others. One might, perhaps, temporarily reduce wages to some extent in certain investment industries if it could be done quickly and once and for all. Building could be stimulated by one decisive cut in building wages. However, I think this would be a risky policy. The knowledge that it is likely to be used might—as soon as a recession has started—lead to expectations that "wages will go down, and before they have done so, I had better sit back and wait and not build." That would intensify the depression, momentarily, at least. On the whole, therefore, I think that relatively stable wage levels create the most favorable conditions for employment. It is true that a relative rise or fall in wages in investment industries compared to the general wage level might be used to check an overexpansion or to stimulate investment, when that is needed. But to attempt this at the appropriate time would seem not to be a practical policy in Western societies.

Should wage rates and wholesale price levels vary quickly, the influence on all kinds of investment will be considerable, and fluctuations in the volume of investment will be inevitable, for people will expect higher or lower prices and will increase or reduce their investment accordingly. Furthermore, consumers' purchases would also be made more erratic, because consumers also would to some extent speculate in what may happen to prices next year or next month.

Now, if consumers reduce their purchases when prices are expected to fall, and the professional investors do the same, that means that planned savings are increased by consumers at the very time when planned investment goes down. It is not very useful that people try to increase savings at a time when investment falls. Then a lack of balance is created and a tendency towards a contraction of economic activity, a recession, is inevitable.

NEED OF A PUBLIC INVESTMENT POLICY

The impression one gains is that some central bank or government action to check the tendency to excesses in the construction trades at one time and stimulate it at other periods is almost certainly necessary, because the influence of changes, say, in marriage rates and in the age composition of population, of movements of people from one part of the country to another, and of technological changes will be so considerable that, unless there is some central interference and control, considerable fluctuation in construction activity will be inevitable.

It goes without saying that it would be useful if business firms were to plan some of their investments of the more durable kind a long time ahead, and if, in so doing, they were not held back—perhaps some of them might even be stimulated—by the expectation of a slight recession six or nine months hence. It is not at all certain that this would be a bad policy from their own point of view.

We all know about the pig cycle. In the twenties, the Danish farmers who increased the number of pigs when prices were low and reduced the number of pigs when prices were high made a lot of money, whereas those who acted in the more normal way of increasing the number when prices were high only got the larger volume ready for sale when prices were falling. I have actually met some businessmen who said they always planned to invest when business conditions were bad. They hoped thus to be ready for better business conditions a couple of years hence. But, that was in the interwar period.

PRIVATE INVESTMENT BY CONSUMERS

I turn now to the question of private investment by consumers. If the wage level were kept relatively stable and if monopoly prices were, on the whole, prohibited by government regulations, then expectations of sudden and considerable price changes with regard to the durable consumer goods need not arise. Moreover, if serious unemployment were not caused by other factors, I suppose consumers would—in most cases—go on buying durable consumer goods at a relatively even rate. Consumers' purchases of durable consumer goods are therefore as a rule rather a secondary element in the process. It is true, of course, that the appearance of "new" types of durable goods might bring a sudden change in demand. There might also be a "reinvestment cycle" with regard to durable consumer goods, just as there has been, for instance, with regard to ships in Norway. In one period shipping companies buy lots of ships and people buy many motor cars; and then, after ten or twenty years, they have to renew this body of ships and cars. But so far I do not know that it has been proved that there has been anywhere a reinvestment cycle in durable consumer goods strong enough to exercise a major influence on employment. There might, however, be one after the Second World War, because the war did prevent people from buying durable consumer goods, and they will buy a lot of them as they become available.

If consumers' purchases of durable consumer goods declined considerably, it might be advisable to change credit conditions. One might—as suggested by Professor Riefler—reduce the initial payments for installment purchases and lengthen the period of amortization, if a stimulus to demand is desirable. On the other hand, if the demand for consumer goods tends to expand too rapidly, one could increase the initial payment and reduce the period of amortization. In the post-war years the Federal Reserve System has been experimenting with varying restrictions on installment credits. One can, of course, also use subsidies in depressions to help people buy durable goods like furniture (see the review of the Swedish program in Chapter 4).

## PUBLIC INVESTMENT AND BUDGET POLICY

The minimum requirement on public investment is that it be kept on a relatively stable level, not varying with the fluctuations in the general business activity and therefore not contributing to them. In Sweden up to 1932 municipal investment and investment in government business enterprises has had a tendency to follow the business cycle. It rose considerably from 1946 to 1948 and thus contributed to the overemployment. This is most unsatisfactory. It is, of course, very important that municipalities and government enterprises should lead in making long-period programs of investment, because they, at least, should be in a position to ignore the risk of a recession.

Secondly, everybody agrees that it would be natural to try to offset to some extent variations in private investment by increases or reductions in public investments, financed through borrowing. One practical and psychological difficulty is how to reduce these public investments quickly enough, once recovery is well under way. It is usually hard to convince the general public and the political assemblies that the time to prepare for cutting down public investment is while unemployment is still considerable. But if a start is not made *then,* before the stage of virtually full employment is reached, public investment may have the harmful effect of intensifying the boom.

As indicated at the beginning of this chapter, the aim of the public investment policy should not be to offset changes in private investment only, and, thus, to stabilize the total volume of investment. The latter should be adapted to changes in the willingness to save, or, to put it another way, to changes in the consumers' purchases for current consumption, with due regard to the expansion of aggregate output. It is quite possible—this is a problem that needs much further statistical investigation—that when a boom has developed and has lasted for some time, consumers tend to grow more optimistic and, therefore, to spend a larger part of their expected income for current consumption; in other words, they plan to save less. If that happens, it is desirable to cut down the volume of investment in this second phase of the recovery. I think it is quite likely that this has been the case in Sweden in the post-war years, when consumers seem to have started to consume relatively more than in 1945. This is actually one reason why it was necessary to cut down the volume of investment in Sweden in 1948 and why it should have been done in 1946 to avoid overemployment. So I do not think this is just a "theoretical" problem to adapt the volume of investment to changes in the willingness to save.

Unfortunately, there is little statistical evidence of the changes in the willingness to save. One can see, for example, that people do not put so much money in the savings bank as they used to; but this is only an indication and not a measure of the change. However, it should not be impossible to make selective, detailed investigations by the use of Gallup polls and similar devices to find out something more definite about current changes in the willingness to save. The information could be gathered quickly enough to be useful in policy-making.

## MEASURES TO AFFECT SAVINGS

It is obvious, though, that policy need not regard willingness to save as a given factor in the problem. One might, through policy, *deliberately change the willingness to save,* because one part of it is the savings or the negative savings done by municipalities and governments. The state and the municipalities may have budget surpluses during booms and deficits during depressions. A tendency in this direction is normal because of the attitude of finance ministers and the lack of flexibility of public expenditure. There is often a surplus on current account in boom times, because the Minister of Finance has been cautious, and a deficit in a depression, because he was not pessimistic enough. But it would seem quite natural to initiate a deliberate policy of having a relatively large surplus in boom times and relatively large deficits in depressions. That is the policy of a cyclical balancing of the budget; or, rather, the cyclical balancing of the budget is one example of such a policy. From this point of view, one reaches the conclusion that government finances, for instance, should have a surplus when it is considered desirable to exercise restrictive influence on the economy as a whole. But a surplus should not be used in order to reduce the government debt in a balanced economic situation as a goal by itself, unless it is offset by measures to stimulate investment.

It is not at all certain that surpluses in booms and deficits in depressions will lead to a balancing of the budget in the long run. It depends on the state of business and the volume of employment chosen as the "normal" point at which to balance the budget. If this is relatively high, the periods of budget surplus will be relatively brief and the total of the surpluses is likely to be smaller than the deficits in the depressed conditions. If the degree of employment at which the budget is balanced is below full employment, then any movement from the balancing point to full employment will be made more difficult through a budget surplus. Dr. Beardsley Ruml has, therefore, proposed as a basic principle of public finances that the budget be balanced in the full-employment state.

One could, if one wanted a policy of this type, increase tax rates or introduce new taxes in excessive booms and reduce taxes when business falls below the desired level. In 1931 I suggested, as a quick way of increasing expenditure, that the Swedish Government should not ask people to pay the amounts on the tax forms but should allow everybody to collect a corresponding amount from the Treasury. But somehow people did not take this very excellent proposal seriously!

A policy of lowering taxes in depressions and increasing them in booms should, I think, be worked out beforehand. Tax systems may also be invented that have a "built-in flexibility," that is, yield large returns in booms and small ones in depressions. To reduce the burden of taxes during a depression, particularly for the poorer groups in society, would seem to be quite natural, once we have given up the idea that we must balance the budget over this very artificial astronomical period of twelve months. I do not mean that it is artificial from an astronomical point of view, but from a budgeting point of view.

Unemployment insurance systems with fixed payments have a tendency in the right direction, because funds are piled up during good times when *unemployment* is low, and money is withdrawn when *employment* is low. The effect would, of course, be even greater, if, as has been suggested, the contributions were raised in good times and reduced in depressions. But unemployment insurance funds of the ordinary sort can only mitigate fluctuations that are nevertheless relatively serious. It will not always exercise a damping influence on them, but may, on the contrary, strengthen the recession tendencies. The degree of employment which represents the average and on which unemployment contributions are based (for example, 90 percent) may be quite an unsatisfactory one. From past experience the social policy workers have found it necessary to assume that such a level of employment is the average they can count on. The volume is usually well above that level at the start of a recessive trend. If the employment is at 96 percent when a recession starts, money will still be pumped into the unemployment insurance fund, while employment recedes from 96 to 94 to 92; and only when it gets below 90 does society get the benefit of a net withdrawal from the fund to expand purchases. So unless the unemployment insurance contributions are based on the assumption of a high level of employment, the policy does not contribute to the desired stability of employment on a relatively high level. It tends to weaken the forces that make for a very serious unemployment, but that is all.

CONSUMPTION VS. SAVINGS

Many economists stress the fact that consumers' demand and consumers' expenditure are more stable than the investment expenditure. They therefore draw the conclusion that one should try to increase the share of income spent on consumption and to reduce saving and investment. That would make for a more stable economic system.

For instance, income could be more evenly distributed. That would reduce savings and increase consumption. I think it is true that somewhat—but not much—weaker tendencies to economic fluctuations would be present in a country where people save and invest very little, because purchases for current consumption are relatively stable. But whether this development with a relatively slow rate of expansion, as would then be the case, is preferable to the risks of a somewhat greater fluctuation in employment, is of course a subjective matter about which scientists can say nothing. It is for the politicians, or rather for the people, to decide.

In my opinion there are many good reasons for wanting a more equal distribution of income. It could be brought about, for instance, by improvement in the education of the children from the poorer groups. But I cannot regard the perhaps somewhat greater instability of employment in a rapidly progressive society as a weighty argument for measures to reduce the rate of progress in order to bring about a more even distribution of income and, thereby, a relatively stable employment. Rather, the very fact that employment stabilization is somewhat more difficult of achievement in a rapidly progressing society should be a challenge to economists and politicians to work out a policy that will nevertheless maintain a reasonable degree of stability.

THE BUSINESS CYCLE THEORY

I shall finally raise a question that has been bothering me a great deal. I have asked myself what has become of the business cycle theory in discussions of employment stabilization. Was business cycle theory in the narrow sense of the word just a superfluous pastime? When we analyze stabilization nowadays, we seem to forget about it.

Business cycle theory is sometimes divided into two parts: the theory of the processes of expansion and contraction, and the theory of the "inevitable turns"—the inevitable maxima and minima in the income and production curves. The theory of expansion and contraction is, I think, used in laying a foundation for any kind of stabilization policy, but what about the theory of the inevitable turns? I am inclined to accept the following answer. If we adapt investment in private industry and public business enterprises on the basis of long-run expectations, and if we adapt it in "non-economical" enterprises—for example, ordinary public works—in such a way that the tendency to acceleration does not lead to large fluctuations in aggregate investment, then it need not differ from the teachings of business cycle theory to say that the points at which the curves turn in a new direction may be to a considerable extent controlled. Anyhow, the outswings can be reduced. One can, however, draw one conclusion from what business cycle theory has taught us. To keep relatively stable wage conditions and relatively stable price levels, and to have a great adaptability in the economic system is not enough. There is an inherent instability in the system, and therefore a deliberate policy on the part of governments, central banks, municipalities, business organizations, and trade unions will be necessary to offset these otherwise inevitable tendencies of the cyclical type.

# 3. International Relations and Economic Stability

I COME NOW to some observations on the international aspects of a policy to maintain a high and stable degree of employment. Of course, almost all sides of international economic relations have a bearing on national income and employment. I can only touch upon a few salient questions.[1]

The question to be illuminated might be put like this: Which parts of the policy concerning international economic relations are particularly important and how shall they be handled, in order to obtain a high and stable employment? However, it may prove advantageous to turn the question around as follows: How can the balance of payment be kept in equilibrium in the long run, while maintaining a relatively full volume of employment? By long-run equilibrium I mean that there is no need of short-term borrowing, of depletion of foreign exchange reserves or gold exports to satisfy the demand for foreign exchange that arises from "legitimate" transactions and not from a speculative flight of capital.

In other words, the object is to keep the balance of payments in equilibrium without the aid of a policy that depresses the national income below reasonably full employment and without a deflation of wage rates that is certainly incompatible with such employment conditions. Mr. Nurkse has well formulated the problem to be solved: "to harmonize the re-

[1]A comprehensive discussion is to be found in *Economic Stability in the Post-War World*, Report of the League of Nations' Delegation on Economic Depressions, Geneva, 1945.

quirements of internal equilibrium with those of external equilibrium."[2] However, as always when discussing "full employment," we must not forget that it matters very much how efficient the employment is. An increase in the volume of employment by 1 percent and a decrease in output per unit of labor by 2 percent is not regarded by most people as an improvement. This means that we cannot disregard the influence of various policies on the international division of labor and trade, for international trade is an important method of increasing the efficiency of production. Thus, the policy we are looking for should not only harmonize internal and external equilibrium to a reasonable degree, it should also be favorable to an expansion of the volume of international trade. In certain situations these purposes may conflict. But, it is, I think, on the whole undoubtedly true that "unless expansion of international trade can be reconciled with a reasonable measure of equilibrium in the balance of payments, it will not long be maintained; it will give place to a severe contraction. In the long run, a large uncorrected disequilibrium in the balance of international payments is a contractionist influence of the first importance."[3]

CAUSES OF MALADJUSTMENTS IN INTERNATIONAL ECONOMIC RELATIONS

I shall group my observations on the subject of appropriate policies under three headings: 1) measures to keep *the maladjustments* as small as possible; 2) measures to adapt *the trade*

[2] See Nurkse; "International Monetary Policy and the Search for Economic Stability," *American Economic Review*, May 1942, p. 569.
[3] H. D. Henderson; *The International Problem*, London, 1946, p. 13.

*balances* of individual countries; 3) the use of balancing *capital transactions* during periods of adaptation.

Let us leave wars out of account, as the specific situations that they bring about hardly lend themselves to a general treatment. As the first cause of a fundamental international maladjustment I should then mention serious economic depressions. They involve a decline in employment in countries where they start and tend to drag other countries too into a similar situation. Hence, the maintenance of a reasonably high level of employment in the leading countries—and the avoidance of large and prolonged stoppages owing to labor conflicts—is essential. Otherwise, other countries develop an import surplus that cannot long be paid for. It is particularly important that the large creditor nations maintain employment. Other countries have very limited resources to pay for the import surplus that will be called forth, if they should maintain a higher degree of employment than the creditor countries. Thus, a depression in the latter will rapidly cause either a depression elsewhere or severe trade restrictions. Unfortunately, even a moderate depression in the United States, the leading creditor country, which is in the possession of almost the whole of the world's monetary gold reserve, will—as pointed out by Nurkse —lead to a considerable decline in its purchases abroad and, thus, throw the balance of payments of other countries out of order, at least if the depression is not accompanied by a sudden increase in the export of long-term American capital. The American imports consist largely of raw materials and are, therefore, sensitive to changes in industrial activity. Furthermore, several imports are of a marginal character. For example, the importation of pulp and newsprint provides the marginal quantity required to satisfy the American consumption and will be more drastically reduced than domestic American output in a moderate depression. Besides, American imports are much influenced by speculative changes in inventories which rise in booms and decline in depressions. For all these reasons, the maintenance of a reasonably high employment in the United States is one prerequisite of world economic stability.

If a depression in the United States and some other countries should nevertheless begin, the effects may be mitigated through an increase in American investment abroad. Unfortunately, the financial position of debtor countries is adversely affected when a depression in the United States has begun to reduce its purchases from the former. Many of the borrowing countries do not have a very stable economic situation anyhow, and it is apt to be further weakened by an American depression. Furthermore, even after a period of adjustment and reconstruction in Europe, political risks in the world are likely to be considerable. Hence, it is impossible to say what hope one can have for a policy of speeding up American capital investments abroad as a method to counteract a tendency to a depression in the United States and to mitigate the effect of the American depression on the balance of payments in other countries. The chances would be increased if an American or an international organization could be created to take care of this problem, or if existing institutions, for instance the International Bank, were vested with this task.

## "ONE WORLD" PROSPERITY NOT ESSENTIAL

It is sometimes said, as one argument in favor of the policy of placing capital abroad, that one country cannot be prosperous if all countries are not prosperous—we are all part of one world, and so on. I personally do not believe that at all. I think we can have prosperity in three-fourths of the world even if the fourth part is poor. The condition is that industry in the former part of the world has adapted itself to a state of little trade with the fourth part of the world. Otherwise, I do not see how Europe and America could ever have been prosperous, as China, for example, has been poor forever. There are many good reasons for an international social policy and we do not need to advance weak arguments in favor of it. It is not true either that wage standards have to be reasonable everywhere in order to make prosperity possible anywhere; still less is it true that to insure a high national income everywhere wage standards should be the same everywhere. But it is true that if investment in backward countries, or in countries with relatively scanty capital supply, could be planned in advance and speeded up in depression periods, it would help both the borrowing countries and the lending countries, partly because sudden fluctuations in employment in some part of the world —rich or poor—tend to have an unfavorable influence everywhere.

In some countries governments take a part of the risk for certain types of capital exports, for example through the use of a credit insurance system. Hence, it would not be out of the question to increase the government's share of the risk and, thus, make conditions more favorable to export business when the recession tendencies have started. But here, as elsewhere, it is very difficult for governments to act quickly enough. The effect may be to stimulate export on credit when the recovery is already well under way.

If capital movements do not play a large role in helping to find suitable fields for investment, at least it is to be hoped that they will not develop in so capricious and harmful a manner as to make economic policy in general very difficult. What happened in 1930–1931, when erratic capital movements were one of the most important causes of the international depression and the breakdown of the international monetary system, should not need to happen again. The new international institutions can no doubt lend valuable assistance in solving such problems. I return now to the main argument.

OVEREMPLOYMENT IS HARMFUL

Evidently it is important to avoid a vicious decline in purchases and incomes anywhere. It is equally important to *avoid an undue expansion*. Over-full employment owing to an excessive volume of investment relative to the willingness to save calls forth a tendency for imports to rise and exports to decline. The import surplus can be regarded as a means of drawing upon current savings from other countries, when current savings at home do not suffice. As indicated in the first chapter, a considerable drain on the gold and foreign exchange reserves is apt to lead to import restrictions and to cause disturbances in other countries. Such restrictions cannot offset precisely that increase in imports of the various goods that is caused by the overexpansion of demand. It is likely to be confined to some goods or to be relatively more severe for them than for others. Hence, the secondary effects in other countries will be of a sort to bring about disturbances and reduced employment.

It goes without saying that autonomous policies of deflation and inflation in important countries, that bring about considerable variations in the general price level, are also unfavorable from the point of view of world stability. Such policies make variations in foreign exchange rates necessary. Besides, deflation is hardly possible without a depressed state of economic activity.

## RAW MATERIAL PRICES AND BUFFER STOCKS

Even if excessive booms and depressions are avoided, technical and climatic changes are apt to lead to large fluctuations in the prices of primary commodities. For countries that depend on the exportation of such goods, the result can be a violent disturbance of the balance of payments, which calls forth the use of import restrictions as well as large declines in incomes and employment. It is, therefore, important for world economic stability that such price fluctuations in primary goods be kept within reasonable limits. This will no doubt be difficult, but not so difficult as one might suppose from past experience. Hitherto the recurrence of general booms and depressions of great severity made the task of stabilizing raw material prices well-nigh impossible to carry out. It may not prove quite so difficult in the future, if general business fluctuations can be mitigated. In my opinion it would be wise to make an organized international effort to keep such price fluctuations within practicable limits as a supplement to domestic economic policies that aim at the maintenance of a reasonably high and stable level of employment. I refer particularly to a paper by Professor W. W. Riefler on an international buffer stock agency, "organized and equipped to purchase, store and sell durable, storable commodities in recurrent demand in such a way as to mitigate fluctuations in their prices, in the employment and income of their producers, and in their costs to fabricators, dealers and distributors."[4] Production controls and export quotas tend to subsidize high cost production, and therefore it is probably not advisable to use direct production controls and export quotas as a means of stabilizing raw material prices. We know what happened to the price of rubber in the 1920s. This experience does not invite us to try a similar policy again. It would be better to have an international buffer stock agency which can buy, store and sell in such a way as to mitigate price fluctuations.

The League's Delegation on Economic Depressions has suggested that this buffer stock agency should buy a raw material at a declared minimum price, a price which is declared in advance, and should also undertake to sell it at a declared maximum price. It would then be generally known that fluctuations would remain within those limits. Whether so simple a formula would be sufficient, only experience can tell.

One condition of a successful policy is, of course, that we have more statistics about commodity stocks in all countries, or most countries, than at present. There is no special reason for assuming that the world output of raw materials should, to a very large extent, vary with the business cycle. So if the producers and middlemen insist on reducing or increasing their stocks with business fluctuations, there is need for an international agency that will act in the reverse manner, in order to mitigate price fluctuations. The stocks will obviously have to vary with the vagaries of output relative to consumption, for example, under the influence of climate, but that is another

[4] "A Proposal for an International Buffer Stock Agency," *Journal of Political Economy*, December, 1946, pp. 5–38.

matter; although it constitutes one reason why the whole thing
would be extremely difficult to carry out. It would be worth
trying, nevertheless.

The economic changes touched upon above as causes of maladjustments in the balance of payments have so far been
studied only with regard to their effect on trade. They may,
however, affect the balance of payments also by calling forth
sudden changes in capital movements. Such changes are apt
to be caused also by many other factors, such as political events.
As long as the world remains politically highly unstable—even
to a lesser extent than today—it will be necessary to make
international capital movements subject to a certain degree
of government control.

### THE ADAPTATION OF TRADE BALANCES

Even the most optimistic view of national economic policies
and international coordination of such policies will hardly lead
one to expect that serious disturbances in the balances of payments of most countries will not appear from time to time.
Therefore, an economic system that is to function well and
permit a relatively stable employment on a high level must
provide for an adaptation of the currents of trade. A lasting
unfavorable change, a decline, say, in the foreign demand for
a country's products, must in most cases be met with some relative cheapening of export goods from that country, and, probably, a relative reduction in the demand for foreign commodities by its inhabitants. One way of bringing this about is to
adapt relative costs and prices as between different countries.
If they have a rising tendency abroad, they may be kept more
stable in countries that have been subject to a decline in the

foreign demand. One of the most important questions for governments and central banks is to find out by what means an influence can be exercised on the cost development without the "aid" of depression and considerable unemployment. This is certainly as yet an unsolved problem in the democracies, where for good reasons governments are reluctant to regulate wage rates.

Another method of adjusting relative costs and supply prices is, of course, to vary the external value of the currency. Without the use of exchange rate variations it is impossible to visualize an international economic system that will avoid deflationary policies so severe as to lead to depressions. From a world point of view a moderate depreciation of a currency to a balanced level is often much better than the maintenance of its excessive external value through the use of import restrictions. It is, therefore, fortunate indeed that the charter of the International Monetary Fund provides for such a policy. However, difficulties of many sorts are likely to arise.

The effect of a relative cheapening of the supply of export goods from countries with a weak balance of payments will to a large extent depend on the elasticity of the foreign demand for their products. Therefore, quantitative restrictions that make purchases insensitive to price reductions—and, within limits, sometimes even to price increases—are from this point of view harmful. So are very high import duties. It is particularly important that the strong creditor nations arrange their trade policies in such a way that their demand for foreign goods has a considerable price elasticity. Unfortunately, this has not been the case in the past so far as the United States is concerned. A considerable reduction of the American tariff—an important first step has been taken as a result of the 1948 Geneva negotiations in connection with the formation of the International Trade Organization (and it is hoped that further progress will be made in the course of the Annécy negotiations in 1949)—would increase the stability of the world economic system. Of course, as I have already indicated above, the maintenance of good business conditions in the United States is also essential, for several reasons. It is important for the maintenance of the American demand for imports. Secondly, if a depression occurred, any increased importation of foreign goods would be blamed for the unemployment, caused mainly by the depression. Import restricting measures would no doubt follow. Besides, the effects of a lowering of the foreign prices on the volume of sales of foreign goods in the United States is much affected by whether or not competing American producers find it necessary to reduce their prices, and this will pend largely on the business situation.

### THE EFFECTS OF QUANTITATIVE RESTRICTIONS

The most controversial of the methods to bring about an adaptation of the trade balances is the use of quantitative restrictions. One disadvantage of this method has already been pointed out. Another is the temptation to vary the quotas suddenly and often, thus creating insecure conditions that increase the risks and impede the expansion of international commerce. My personal belief is that what is taught in the orthodox textbooks about equilibrium in international trade still holds good. Given a reasonable period of adjustment and considerable liquidity reserves, I see no reason why relative cost adjustments and orderly moderate changes in the foreign exchange rates should not as a rule be sufficiently effective, at least if creditor countries have moderate tariff walls, no quantitative restrictions, and a relatively high degree of employment. Destruction and disorganization as a result of wars may, of course, make a long period of adaptation necessary. I certainly do not share the view that import restrictions are always "defensive" and legitimate, when they aim at the maintenance or restoring of equilibrium in the balance of payments. If the cause of the weakness of the balance is overemployment, the natural remedy is not import restriction but a policy that will restore the internal balance, through a cut in investment or an increase in savings or both. Besides, it would be unwise to neglect entirely the possibility of a relative cost adjustment. In my opinion, the rules of behavior laid down for international economic policies should emphatically call for such an adjustment when it can be carried out without a deflation that will reduce the volume of employment *seriously* below a full employment state.

Sometimes a country with a weak balance of payments must choose between *exchange depreciation* and *trade restrictions*. The first principle then would seem to be to use a variation in the exchange rates, if there is a reasonable certainty that the factors causing the weak balance are lasting. In other cases, temporary increases in import duties will often be sufficient. Thus, the scope for the legitimate use of quantitative import restrictions would seem to be rather small. In this respect I find the ideas behind the International Trade Organization entirely sound. This conclusion, however, will hold only for a world economic situation in which the fundamental maladjustments due to World War II have been corrected and in which serious economic depressions are prevented. In such a situation one will, I think, be able to do without those bilateral trade agreements based on import and export quotas that are unfortunately necessary in the world today.

No obligation to abstain from using quantitative restrictions as a method of strengthening the balance of payments can, of course, rest upon any country, if other large nations pursue a policy that makes the maintenance of full employment and unrestricted imports incompatible. If in large parts of the world a policy of deflation and depression were to be pursued, disturbances elsewhere would be so considerable that extraordinary measures (as the use of quotas) would be called for and justified. No country has a right to "export its own depression" by selling more and buying less and, thus, creating a surplus in its own balance of payments. A policy that causes a depression in a country with a strong trade balance would make that country the "villain of the piece" and justify defense measures abroad. A standard of behavior of this sort would help to bring about an international coordination of national "business cycle policies" in different countries that should be one of the cornerstones of the postwar international economic system.

The measures taken by individual countries to keep their balance of payments in order will in many cases not be immediately effective. This is true of all such measures except quantitative import restrictions. Hence, if the use of these restrictions is to be limited as much as possible, because of the unfavorable effects and the risk of abuse, it is important that each country should possess a liquidity reserve of gold or foreign exchange and should be willing to use it as a temporary stopgap. However, it is unlikely that—even after the period of transition and correction of war-caused maladjustments—all countries will be in a sufficiently liquid international position. Unless an international financial "Red Cross" or "fire brigade" is able to function and to act rapidly, the chances of avoiding unfortunate policies and considerable employment variations caused thereby would seem to be slight. Fortunately, it is one of the main tasks of the International Monetary Fund to cope with this problem. To some extent the difficulties may be reduced by international capital movements that may come into being after a conceivable political appeasement in the world.

It goes without saying that the chances of obtaining national economic policies with regard to the balances of payment of the type here indicated can be much enhanced by the discussions of the International Trade Organization and the pressure this organization may bring to bear on recalcitrant countries.

### POST-WAR TRANSITION PROBLEMS

The setting I have assumed for the problem in the preceding analysis is better balanced than the one likely to prevail in the world during the next few years. Let me add some brief remarks only on the special problem that is due to the existence of specific maladjustments during that period. With regard to the balance of payments position in 1948, the most characteristic element is the almost universal "dollar scarcity." It should not be overlooked, however, that most countries have a universal "scarcity" of almost all kinds of foreign exchange. This simply means that they would like to buy from abroad more goods than they can pay for through exports and other credit items. The cause of this situation is primarily the state of overemployment—an unbalanced domestic economy—in which the sums people are anxious to spend each year on consumption and investment exceed the value of the current output at existing prices. (See Chapter 1.) A contributory and important cause is, of course, the fact that commodity stocks—the working capital—were seriously reduced in many belligerent countries and have not yet been refilled, and that much machinery is on the verge of being worn out in the absence of normal replacement. Besides, Great Britain and other countries have spent a large share of their foreign investments to finance the war and an adaptation to the loss of dividends and interest payments will take time. The actual destruction of productive machinery through bombing is probably far less important than the disruption of trading connections, the disappearance of incomes from foreign investment and of certain sources of supply (for example, Germany), and similar aftereffects of the war. The fact that a country like Sweden is in a position similar to that of many former belligerent countries indicates, however, that the state of overinvestment and overemployment is probably the most important cause. To some extent, the above-mentioned direct effects of the war are just an explanation why it has proved so "tempting" in formerly belligerent countries to attempt an investment policy beyond their capacity—with a weak balance of payments as a consequence. However, the war effects are also a direct cause of a very insistent need of foreign goods, as raw materials to refill the pipe lines and reduce bottlenecks. The dollar scarcity arises chiefly because the United States, in an economic world of this sort, 1) has an industrial apparatus that has not been damaged but expanded during the war; 2) has avoided overinvestment; 3) has a tariff of considerable height. Hence, the American demand for foreign goods is less insistent than the foreign demand for American goods.

In a situation of this kind it is improbable that a depreciation of the currencies would *alone* be able to reestablish the balance. In many countries like France and Sweden, costs and prices are in 1948 on a relatively higher level than in the United States, and a rise of the dollar in terms of their currencies is called for. The same may be true of the relation between dollar and sterling. But it is unlikely to be sufficient for a restoration of an international equilibrium between the United States and Western Europe. For example, the influence of depreciation on exports to the United States, say, from Great Britain is difficult to predict. The all-round development of American industry and the character of American tariff policy make it improbable that a price reduction for British goods in terms of dollars by 10 or 15 percent would increase the *value* of the British exports to the United States by as much as, say, 50 percent during the next few years. Hence, the dollar scarcity cannot be decisively alleviated during so brief a period by the simple means of a policy of depreciation of the pound. Other things are required also. For the time being, the use of quantitative import restrictions is impossible to avoid. How severe the restrictions need to be will naturally depend largely on the size of the American lending and relief action called the "Marshall Plan"—which I cannot refrain from calling an act of extraordinary foresight and generosity.

THE DOMESTIC BALANCE

The problem remains what kind of national and international economic policies will be most likely to favor a transition to a more balanced world economy. An increase in production everywhere is the most obvious thing to be desired.

Organized action like the Marshall Plan can do much to prevent undernourishment and eliminate bottlenecks as well as reintroduce Germany into the international economy. Domestic action to get rid of bottlenecks, for example through increased output of coal, is also vital. But, all such measures will fail to solve the problem if they are not accompanied by a restoration of the fundamental balance in the domestic system in the various countries. An equilibrium between the demand for goods and the current supply—a return from a state of overemployment to a balanced employment—is called for. The way to achieve it is to keep the total value of investment within the limits set by the willingness of the people to save. To the extent that a transfer of labor and other productive resources from the investment industries to industries producing for consumption and export is not possible, a reduction in consumption relative to income, that is, an increase in saving, is the only possible method.

A second condition of a development in the direction of international equilibrium is that costs and supply prices in countries with a weak balance of payments are kept relatively low compared with in the financially strong countries, with due regard to the foreign exchange rates. A method of approaching the practical handling of this problem may be very briefly indicated. If the situation before the war is taken as a basis, an index of the rise in costs—largely consisting of wages—can be computed for each country and a "purchasing power parity" arrived at. The most difficult process involved is, of course, to allow for the changes in efficiency and, thus, to compute a "revised parity." The currencies of countries with a weak balance and relatively less favorable terms of trade than before the war will have to be kept below this revised purchasing power parity. However difficult and arbitrary such measurements may seem, there is probably no other way to find guidance with regard to the proper and practical relation of other currencies to the dollar. It is to be hoped that the International Monetary Fund or a special agency of the European Economic Cooperation Organization will attack this problem.

A third and important step that would help to recreate international balance would be to increase the elasticity in the American demand for foreign commodities and services. As already indicated a lowering of the American tariff would be helpful. This would particularly be the case if American industry adapted itself to the fact that certain kinds of products should normally be supplied from abroad. In other words, a certain change in the structure of American industry is required. Otherwise, a claim for a return to higher protection is certain to come as soon as some recession in the general business situation sets in. The special clause proposed in 1947 for insertion in all American bilateral agreements to reduce trade barriers—under the banner of the International Trade Organization—would greatly increase the risk of such a development. This clause refers to the case when an American industry is damaged by the importation of foreign goods on which the tariff has been reduced, and stipulates complete freedom of action—to increase the tariff again—in such cases.

## THE EQUAL TREATMENT PRINCIPLE

The fourth and last factor I shall mention is the desirability of a modification of the equal-treatment principle during the period of transition. In the next few years the dollar scarcity will compel many countries to cut American imports by means of quota restrictions. Should they therefore—assuming that they have obtained an agreement with the United States based on "equal treatment"—be forced to reduce imports of the same goods from other countries *by the same percentage* compared with pre-war figures, an unnecessary reduction of world trade would follow. It would reduce the ability of European countries to help one another and increase the need of American assistance! It is, therefore, a practical problem of the greatest importance to devise methods through which additional trade between weak currency countries can be allowed and fostered, without restricting in any way the trade between such countries and the United States. The volume of the latter trade is, on the whole, determined by the American willingness to buy foreign goods (including tourists' expenditures) and to lend capital abroad. The trade between weak currency countries can be developed without diverting productive resources from their production of goods for the American market, which they are most anxious to supply. Thus, there is in the present situation little risk that a modification of the equal-treatment principle would be harmful to American industry. It would certainly be helpful for reconstruction in the world at large. This fact has been to some extent recognized by American trade policy, for example, in bilateral treaties with Great Britain and Sweden.

It would be very optimistic indeed to expect that a restoration of a relatively free international trade can be effected in the next three or four years. It seems unlikely that a general economic balance in the domestic economy can be restored in all countries. Prices and wages will rise with greater speed in some countries than in others, and the tendency to overemployment will be strong in the former group but weaker or absent in the other group. A consistent liberal American trade policy based on a deliberate adaptation of American industry to the international situation also seems, alas, far from certain. Under such conditions foreign exchange rates now here, now there, will be out of balance. The elimination of most of the quantitative trade restrictions in a milieu of this sort in a few years' time seems out of the question. Furthermore, the use of such restrictions will be necessary in many countries to prevent a lack of certain international means of payment—as gold or dollars—from limiting the possibilities of trade in other channels unnecessarily. Thus, to draw up lines between useful and legitimate trade policies, on the one hand, and vicious and illegitimate policies, on the other, will be extraordinarily difficult. The International Trade Organization will have a formidable task.

# 4. A Swedish Program for Anti-Depression Measures

IN JANUARY, 1933, about two years after the investigations of its employment policy had been started, the Swedish Government presented a budget proposal with an Appendix prepared by Professor Myrdal on fiscal policy and depressions. Professor Myrdal's argument followed a line that was at that time generally accepted by the younger generation of Swedish economists. He advocated an attempt to create an adequate volume of aggregate demand through an increase in public works, financed through borrowing. A policy of this sort had been proposed both by politicians and economists in 1932, but the arguments in favor of it had been less fully developed than in Myrdal's memorandum.

The Swedish Riksdag in the spring approved a large expansion of public works. The wonderful results of this policy have been described even by some foreign economists. It is true that Sweden had a remarkable recovery in the two or three years following, but I am very sorry that I have to state as my opinion that this policy did not succeed very well, because it was put into effect too late.

From the spring of 1933 to February, 1934, a labor conflict occurred in the building and construction industries. Obviously it is hard to start public works when you cannot build; so instead of the increase in the sum of private and public investment that had been decided upon, what we got was a reduction in the volume of construction. A revival of industry, nevertheless, started in 1933 owing to the stimulus of an increased foreign demand for Swedish products. In 1934 the expansion of the foreign demand for export goods, including pulp and timber, had already brought about a considerable amelioration of the economic situation. Then the government investment financed by borrowing was speeded up and, no doubt, somewhat increased the pace of the recovery. It was not a large sum that was spent—about 200,000,000 kronor in twelve months, corresponding in the United States, on the basis of wealth and income, to $1,500,000,000.

I should like to mention, in passing, that there was one fundamental difference between the policy that was planned in Sweden and the one that was tried in the United States in the same period, namely with regard to wage policy. Half of the economists who worked out the theory of "expansion" in Sweden were members of the Socialist Party, so there was certainly no political bias behind the idea that it is not useful in the beginning of a depression to raise the nominal wage level. The thing to increase when you want to expand employment is the aggregate demand *in terms of wage units,* in terms of the pay the worker obtains for one day of work, because then people can buy goods "containing" more days of work and employment will grow. It is, a priori, very unlikely that the sale of something can be increased by raising the price—unless expectations of a further rise in price are caused. As a general rule one will not increase the sale of anything by raising its price. This becomes obvious in the case of a small unit. Assume that we want to raise the purchases of a commodity such as bread or tea. Nobody would dream of recommending a higher price for bread or tea. But if the price is raised on a very large thing, like labor in general, then the increase in price will be to a considerable extent offset by the increase in demand resulting from the higher income. It is only when the price of everything —of output as a whole—is increased that you get a balance; you increase the supply price and demand about equally, if savings are not affected.

To return to the Swedish policy, in 1935, the Unemployment Commission published its final report based on theoretical investigations made by several economists on "the economics of unused resources." It was a very detailed report, containing what even today seems to stand out as a relatively complete analysis of various aspects of the policy against unemployment. It deals in equal detail with the purchasing power aspects, the organization of the labor market and the monopolistic price policies, and somewhat more briefly with the international economic aspects. The first practical result of a more permanent character of the new "expansionist" attitude was a decision made in 1937 by the Swedish Riksdag that no attempt should be made to balance the budget over a twelve-month period. There is no a priori economic reason why the state should be forced to employ a twelve-month period as a basis for balancing its accounts. The Swedish Riksdag accepted a proposal to take a business cycle as the basic period, although this proposal was based on a report by a committee including half the Swedish professors of economics. These professors managed to agree, which is supposed to be rare. Under the government aim at balancing the budget over a period including a business cycle—whatever that may be— the budget normally should have a deficit in depressions and a surplus in booms. In order to prevent the Minister of Finance from forgetting the deficit in a past depression, rules were laid down that if a deficit appeared one year, he must enter 20 percent of that deficit as a debit item to be covered by revenue in the next year. If a deficit arose in the second year too, the government should put as an item to be covered by income during the third year 40 percent of the annual deficit (20 percent of the first deficit and 20 percent of the second). By applying this rule, it was hoped to remove a deficit from the world eventually. The 20 percent rule is not a very rational thing, of course. However, it placates the conservative opinion, and the whole thing went through in the Riksdag without any opposition at all. Unfortunately, the scheme was not practiced because the war came along. It is true that in 1938–39 we had a certain budget surplus, but then during the war we had enormous deficits owing to huge expenditures for defense purposes. Now, in the years after the war we again have certain surpluses. Whether they are large enough to satisfy the requirements in accordance with the financial principles adopted in 1937 is perhaps doubtful. The budget surplus for the year 1946–47—measured as the difference between actual expenditure on current account, excluding investment in state owned business enterprises and other capital expenditure, and the actual income—was about 400,000,000 kronor, but would have been almost twice that sum—700,000,000 kronor—if a change in the bookkeeping had not taken place. If you take into account the difference in the national income, this would correspond in the United States to about $7,000,000,000—a relatively large sum. The surplus was partly due to the pronounced state of overemployment and by far exceeded expectations. In 1947–48 the surplus exceeded 500,000,000 kronor.

I return again to the pre-war policy. In 1938 there was an-other result of the new attitude: a legislation that enables firms to set aside part of their profits into special funds, tax free, on condition that those sums will be spent in buildings and con-struction during a period which the government declares to be a suitable period—usually something of a depression. If the money is not spent in the course of the period when the gov-ernment has said, "Now we have a time when it is desirable to invest," then the firms must pay the normal tax, plus 3 per-cent annual interest from the time when the fund was created.

Why is it laid down that the money should be invested in buildings and construction? Because investment in machines may be completely written off tax free any way, any year the firm so desires. Thus, business firms do not pay taxes on the profit, which they can dispose of by writing off machinery. As to inventories, these also can be written down tax free to a very low figure.

PLANNING PUBLIC WORKS

In 1944 a report was presented by a special public in-vestment board that had been created a few years earlier in order to prepare detailed plans for public works. It had been found in the thirties in many cases that it took much time before public works could get under way. The conclusion was drawn that all the blueprints should be ready in advance. Therefore, these blueprints have been made, and now quite a large volume of public works is ready for realization whenever a recession starts. The financial technique used was the follow-ing one: over and above the ordinary current budget and the ordinary capital and investment budget, the government prepared a third, "an emergency budget," which includes grants for all these planned extra public works. The Riksdag has to pass each appropriation individually, just as if it had been an ordinary proposal, but nothing is to be done about it until the day when the government thinks that now is the time when the general economic situation calls for an expansion of public investment. Then it has only to press a button and the whole thing starts.

The budget for 1945–46, the first to include this particular device, covered public works and subsidies to municipal works amounting to 600,000,000 kronor, which in the United States would correspond to an expenditure of about $6,000,000,000. If one takes into account that this includes only a part of the cost of the municipal investments, it means that new public investment amounting to a somewhat larger figure can be obtained relatively quickly. In the last years the "emergency budget" has not been presented to the Riksdag, the assumption being that there will be time enough to get it passed by the Riksdag when signs of a slackening of business appear and before a serious recession has developed.

Some people have expressed the opinion that the state and municipalities cannot put off useful investments on any large scale. There is a great deal of truth in that, but I think it is an exaggeration. It is possible to make out a list of investments which are regarded as useful but which for various reasons one does not want to carry out in a certain year under ordinary conditions, but which will probably be made in one of the following years. These investments are entered in the emergency budget. When the first year has passed without a depression, the most urgent of the investments are to be taken out of the emergency budget and put into the ordinary capital investment budget for the second year. Then some new things are put into the emergency investment budget so there is always a sufficient reserve of works to be done—public buildings, and schools, and investments in railroads, postal offices, telegraph offices (such public utilities are in Sweden run by the state).

There is also a scheme for increasing subsidies for agriculture and forestry during depressions. We have an old policy of state contribution to a farmer who wants to improve the drainage system or raise the productivity of the forests, a policy somewhat similar to the American soil conservation program. Under depressed conditions the government will increase such subsidies so as to make people speed up that kind of investment.

A NEW STAGE IN PUBLIC FINANCE

Some people think that such measures as changes in public investments financed by borrowing will always be too small to exercise any considerable influence on business conditions. I cannot share this view. I think my colleague, Professor Myrdal, is quite right when he says that we have passed through two stages of public finance and into a third stage that requires a different kind of thinking in these matters. The first stage was when the state expenditure was so small compared with the national income that the Minister of Finance adapted the revenue from taxation to his expenditure without having to consider any reactions from taxation on the economic system as a whole. That was before 1914. Then, in the period between the two wars, we drifted into a system under which public expenditure became so large a part of the total national expenditures that its variations substantially affected the volume of national income and expenditure. That is where we have been, most of us, in our thinking. But in the third stage into which we have drifted—at least in some European countries (I make no predictions about a possible future large reduction of defense expenditures in the United States that might reverse the tendency)—the public expenditure has become so large a share of the total national expenditure that its variations can become one of the dominating factors in the whole economic development as well as in the course of the "business cycle."

We have in Sweden in 1948 a net national income of about twenty-two billion kronor. The public expenditure, after the deduction of sums that appear twice, is something like five and a half billions or a little more. This does not include capital expenditure in state or municipal undertakings or enterprises. Hence, the expenditure directly controlled by the state or state enterprises and the municipalities runs in the neighborhood of seven billion kronor. This is a very considerable share of the national revenue. Government finance, therefore, has to be studied with regard to its effect on the economic system as a whole. I think it is the accepted view in Sweden that the state should not start repaying its debt just because it has grown in the preceding years; it should be repaid only if that would be helpful in causing a deflationary tendency needed as a check on inflation or exaggerated booms, as in the last few years. If there is already, for other reasons, a tendency towards a depression, it would be irrational to reduce a war debt, through a budget surplus, and thereby intensify the depression.

In the early part of 1944, the Swedish Post-War Economic Planning Committee started its work. I shall try to describe now some of the more important proposals made by this committee; using therefor not only the official reports but also an article by the Secretary, Professor Kock, since 1947 member of the government, and a memorandum by one of the experts, Professor Svennilsson.

Before coming to the concrete problems, I should like to characterize the attitude taken by this committee. It fixed as the goal for the employment policy *a high and steady level of employment,* as far as possible, in the ordinary lines of occupation. It is true that the structural changes in industry must be considered, but with that reservation, the goal should be to keep people employed wherever they normally work. The possibility of structural changes makes it, of course, very important that there be a sufficient mobility of labor, improved labor exchanges and training schemes.

If public policy is to achieve the desired effect, a coordination of measures influencing different fields of economic activity is required. Therefore the most important aspect of the work of this committee is its presentation of a great variety of measures that can be combined in such a way as to fit the requirements of special situations as they arise.

In Sweden the depressions seem to have been "imported from abroad." The country is not large enough to create depressions of its own, so they spread to Sweden partly through a reduction in the foreign demand for Swedish goods. Therefore, it must be an essential part of any Swedish anti-depression policy to maintain production in the export industries, in spite of the drop in foreign demand. If that could be achieved, the committee says, that is, if the volume of income, including unemployment benefits, in export and in investment industries, can be maintained, then no serious reduction need be feared in the consumption industries that are working chiefly for the home market. A tacit assumption is, I think, made that the general wage level will not be reduced and therefore there will be no considerable fall in the price of consumer goods which might induce consumers to curtail their purchases suddenly.

It is unlikely, however, that in a country like Sweden where the normal value of exports is as large as 15–20 percent of the national income, a reduction in the income in export industries and investment trades can be completely avoided in the case of a world-wide depression. Therefore, other measures are needed to create expansionist tendencies offsetting the tendencies to contraction that come from the reduction in these industries and trades. The offsetting measures should be directed to increase consumers' demand to avoid a large transfer of workers from consumer industries into public works. Public works are regarded only as one of many different measures that together make up a policy against a slump, for public works cannot easily and usefully be expanded beyond a certain point.

The consumer demand that tends to fall in depressions is particularly the demand for durable and semidurable goods, furniture, motor cars, refrigerators and radios, household articles, textiles, clothing, and shoes. It happens that there are large unsatisfied needs for such goods in most countries, partic-

ularly where the standard of living is not so high as in the
United States. For instance, it was found in the early thirties
that a very large proportion of the children in Sweden did
not have beds of their own. This was rather a dark picture,
surprising even to people who knew social conditions in Sweden. What could be more useful as an investment than to see
to it that the children got beds of their own? Hence, it is natural to make an attempt to increase the purchases of durable
and semidurable consumer goods in case of a recession. This,
the committee suggests, can be done through a *temporary* increase in the aid that is given to families with children. In the
last ten years Sweden has built up a permanent "population
policy," for the purpose of equalizing to some extent the standard of living between families with children and families without children. It takes the form of a cash grant ($70) without
"means test" to all children below sixteen years of age, special
pensions to "widows' children" and orphans, grants to reduce
house rent, free school luncheons, schoolbooks, medical care,
and so on. The regular house-rent subsidy given to families
with two or more children is 10 percent of the rent for each
child—maximum 50 percent—plus some other benefits. Beginning with the second form of the secondary schools, sti-
pends of about $140 are given without any "means test" to
each child who lives outside of the town where the school is
located. In addition an extra stipend up to a maximum of
$155 is given, after a "means test," to school children whether
or not they live where there is a secondary school.

Why not introduce a business cycle aspect into this permanent population policy, and, during depressions, increase the
benefits given to families with children? The Committee sug-

gested a temporary grant to families with children to cover a part of the costs for purchases of durable consumer goods in case of a depression. In other words, it is a combination of the ordinary social and the special anti-depression policies.

The government expenditure for social purposes, except unemployment benefits, has often been reduced in times of depression in Sweden and elsewhere. Now, this is all wrong, the Committee thinks. The social expenditure should be increased at a time when society can afford it, that is, when it makes for a better utilization of resources. Therefore, plans for new social reforms should be worked out as early as possible, and if a depression comes, the realization of these new social reforms should be hastened.

Here, as elsewhere, the idea behind the Swedish proposals is not the Keynesian one of the danger of a *permanent* underemployment and the need of some policy to maintain investment on a sufficiently high level. We are, in this respect, old-fashioned in Sweden. The proposed policy was, in 1944-45, based on the assumption that there are business cycle movements and that, in certain periods, we will probably have a tendency towards too large employment, an assumption justified by the development in 1946-48.

After this general introduction, let me try to make a brief survey as to some of the proposals of this committee. I shall not now go into what had already been decided before the war—the cyclical balancing of the budget and the investment fund legislation, the scope of which may be extended to some degree.

The Committee emphasizes the need of a coordination of the public and private investment. Therefore, it suggests the

creation of an advisory council that will help towards a voluntary coordination of the two. It is essential that in so far as
possible investments be directed into productive channels, that
is to say, those that will increase efficiency, and that they do
not set up maladjustments. Hence, the investment policy must
be based on a distinction between primary causes of depressions and secondary reactions.

As to the *municipal* investments, the Committee is not very
optimistic. It is afraid that it will be difficult to do more than
bring them on an even keel. For various reasons, many municipal investments are closely bound up with the state of business—traffic, the sale of electricity in a city, the sale of gas,
and so on—but the municipalities should be required to
achieve a fairly even volume of investment and not to vary it
with business cycles, as they have done hitherto, as a rule. The
state can encourage this not only by persuasion, but also because it is financing a part of the municipal investment in
Sweden, as in many other countries. Besides, the municipalities
cannot borrow without permission from the Treasury.

As to *private* investments, the Committee recommends that
attempts be made to counteract their tendency to fall when
there is a recession, and to expand some of them. An investment council of the Swedish sort set up in 1946 can help to
bring about a voluntary coordination. Representatives of industry and trade sit in the council together with representatives of the government, and persuasion is brought to bear
upon them. One can persuade people to do a great deal. Secondly, there are the possibilities of government stimulus to
private investment, e.g., by means of tax measures. Thirdly,
there is a possibility of a direct control of private building and

construction, a control created during the present state of over-employment and post-war scarcities. However, the Committee thinks it is inadvisable to retain this as a permanent policy in its strict form, retaining only that part of the control necessary to even out the seasonal variations in the building and construction trade.

### USE OF CREDIT POLICY TO INFLUENCE INVESTMENT

Fourthly, interest and credit policies can be used to affect private investment. That is something that one is almost surprised to read about in the post-war period, because it is so little fashionable to talk about interest policy.

The Committee emphasizes the fact that as a rule it is cheaper to invest in depression times—one reason why it may prove possible to persuade businessmen to invest more than they would have done when the old way of thinking ruled. Moreover, businessmen will do what they can to forestall state intervention. Therefore, they are likely to respond to the suggestion that, if they "behave well" without compulsion, they may avoid it altogether. As a result of the growing and long-lasting scarcity of labor in recent years, businessmen have become anxious to keep their labor force together; that is one reason why they might be inclined to increase investment in a depression when they cannot keep all their workers employed in normal production. Business organizations can exert an influence in this respect through information and propaganda. They should, however, consider not only the time element but also the localization of industry, the problem of unemployment has a great deal to do with *where* industrial activity is slackening and *where* there are possibilities of expanding it. The Federation of Swedish Industry has created a special institute for advice with regard to the localization of industry.

The Committee emphasizes that business firms should be encouraged to keep their assets sufficiently liquid so that they will not be forced to reduce their investments. This is one reason why there has been no talk about changing those of our tax laws which permit business firms to consolidate their position through the writing down of machines and inventions, tax free.

I have already mentioned that the government can vary the subsidies to private investment in agriculture and forestry, but the Committee does not want this policy expanded to include manufacturing industries.

As to housebuilding, it would not have been surprising if the recommendation had been made to expand it in depressions, for its volume is very much influenced by the government. From 1947 the Swedish Government has financed housebuilding to a large extent. Loans are advanced to municipalities and similar organizations up to 100 percent of the cost. However, the investigations made by the special committee for housebuilding have shown that it is better to aim at a stable volume of housebuilding in the cities, because if the labor force in the building industries has been expanded, it is very difficult to contract it again, except very slowly. The building industry is a high-wage industry, and workers who have been used to earning almost twice as much per hour as they get elsewhere are unwilling to leave it. Out in the country, on the other hand, one can expand building in a depression, because, later on, workers drift back into other pursuits more easily.

ORGANIZATION OF INVESTMENT COUNCIL

This council includes one member of the government who presides and representatives of the special board for public investments, the labor market board, the permanent house-building finance board, the manufacturing industries, the employers' organization, the workers' trade unions, the cooperative movement, the retail trade, and the wholesale trade. The head of the Business Cycle Institute is present as an expert, and of course there are other experts also.

The council is a forum for discussion to work out the policy needed in each stage of development. Its object is to influence the volume of private investment and to bring about a coordination of private investment with public investment. For obvious reasons no majority decisions are made. An effort is made to reach voluntary agreements which each party tries to bring into effect in its own sphere of action. The council may also express opinions publicly, in order to influence the policies of the various groups in society.

During the years of overemployment in 1946–48 the council has taken a very passive attitude and has played only a minor role.

EXPORT INDUSTRIES INVENTORIES

Another proposal made by the post-war planning committee is state stimulus to increase inventories in depressions, particularly in the export industries. It must be remembered that the export industries are very important in the Swedish economy. It is not desirable that a large number of the workers should be temporarily transferred to public works during a depression. What then can one do? It is not practicable to make us read newspapers that are twice the normal size in order to consume the newsprint in Sweden when exports thereof decline; nor can we use in other ways all the pulp that we normally export, or any large part of it. In some cases, however, it is possible to manufacture export goods and pile them up in stocks. It has been found that in the first stage of a depression inventories will often rise; but in the second stage they may go down. I have been told that some recent investigations made in the United States support that opinion. This development is only natural because a long depression breeds pessimism and makes businessmen reduce their supply of liquid capital.

Swedish businessmen agreed it might be a good thing to produce commodities for stocks and pile up inventories in a depression; but some of them said that the knowledge that these stocks exist would reduce the world market prices. For instance, if Sweden had large stocks of pulp, foreign buyers would pay a lower price for it. To this the economists replied: "There is a certain supply and a certain demand that is independent of Swedish policy. As long as the stocks are being maintained, supply is not affected by their existence. How can the stocks influence price? Only when the boom period comes and the stocks are sold will prices be maintained on a lower and healthier level than would otherwise be the case." The exporters answered that the stocks would affect prices "psychologically" the whole time. If the foreign buyers know that the stocks are there, the outcome will not only be lower prices when the stocks are put on the market in the boom conditions, but prices under more "normal periods" will be lower than they would otherwise have been. Thus, the result will be a lower average price over the whole cycle.

After all, even if this should be the case, to a certain extent it need not mean a loss to the Swedish economy. A lower average price will be natural if production is kept on a higher average level. Such a policy may well be an advantage not only to buyers but also to the exporting country. It all depends on the extent to which world market prices react. Besides it will be useful for the exporters to be more nearly able to satisfy foreign demand than has hitherto been usual in boom times. Secondly, it may be useful from the point of view of home supply to have stocks of certain goods, for instance of timber. If Great Britain had piled up a stock of coal, it would have been quite useful in the coal crisis of February, 1947. Obviously there are advantages in creating a reserve in slack times, particularly in industries with very good export possibilities in the boom times.

Can the state bring about this increase in inventories? A government agency could purchase part of the goods, pile them up, and sell them later. But it is considered more natural for the state to grant certain credits at low interest rates, although not so low that there is an element of subsidy in the credit terms. In some instances, the state can give a guarantee to carry part of the eventual loss on the inventories without asking for part of any profit that might accrue.

The Committee recommended that Sweden should, during the last period of the war and the first period after the war, make use of its productive capacity to pile up stocks. This was actually done to some extent on the initiative of the firms concerned. The stocks of pulp and timber were unusually large at the end of the war. This was a natural thing to do without any state guarantee, because everybody could see that there would be a large foreign demand for such goods after the war.

An investigation has been made as to the existence of a surplus capacity in Swedish industry, in order to define somewhat more clearly the limit to this kind of policy. The Committee has suggested that a special board be created to take charge of the matter and to study marketing conditions in greater detail, but that board has so far not been appointed.

STIMULATING SALE OF DURABLE CONSUMER GOODS

Having already mentioned the proposed measures to stimulate the sale of durable consumer goods, I will cite a few facts about another proposal made by the Committee. Families with at least two children under sixteen years of age, plus widowed or unmarried mothers with one child or more, should receive a subsidy in the form of a discount of 50 percent of the price when clothes, furniture, and household goods (including kitchen equipment and so on) are purchased at the proper times, that is, in depression periods. There should be no means test. The subsidies should be limited to the basic sum of 50 kronor in each case, plus 25 kronor for each child. That would mean that a family with three children could get 125 kronor or approximately $35. The annual cost has been estimated at 64 million kronor, if every one eligible availed himself of the subsidy. That would correspond to $640,000,000 in the American economy. The Committee thinks that it will be possible to get an extra advantage if production of standard qualities is organized in large series, similar to the advantages achieved in Great Britain during the war through "utility goods." Furthermore, there would be new possibilities for a control of the quality of the commodities by a special research institute. That institute should also try to educate the recipients of the subsidy to spend it for useful goods.

To organize this policy a special board is proposed, which should also investigate the advisability of changing the credit conditions for installment purchases with business fluctuations. The board should also investigate the possibilities of persuading the government and municipal institutions to buy durable goods in the depression. If they need to replace old office furniture, they should, as far as possible, buy it in depression times.

### SEASONAL CHANGES IN EMPLOYMENT

The post-war planning Committee also occupied itself with the problems of seasonal unemployment, but that work was taken over by the Department of Commerce, with the aid of special committees for individual industries. Some private industries had already tackled the problem on their own initiative. For example, the shoe industry organized measures to avoid seasonal unemployment by agreeing, for example, that salesmen from the shoe factories would only visit retailers in certain periods each year. Retailers are discouraged from sending in rush orders at the last minute, necessitating overtime work and extra labor, with a consequent reduction in employment later. The new policy has at once reduced seasonal unemployment in the shoe industry to a fraction of its former figure. The existence of over-full employment in general has made the shoe manufacturers anxious to provide an even employment to avoid the risk of the migration of workers to other industries.

### INCREASING EMPLOYMENT BENEFITS IN DEPRESSIONS

Another of the Committee's proposals was not received in a very friendly fashion; as a matter of fact, it was turned down even by Socialists in the city of Stockholm and in the unemployment board and various other institutions. This proposal was that unemployment cash benefits should be increased in times of depression. The Committee's argument was as follows: In normal times cash benefits should not be raised to the level of the normal wage, lest unemployed persons have no inducement to find a job. But in a severe depression there are no jobs, so why not then give the unemployed almost a full wage? Space does not permit detailed discussion of this curious project here. I dare say that retailers whose income shrinks in a depression cannot understand why a man who is out of work should get more money when everyone else is getting less. Moreover, the cash benefits to the unemployed in high-wage industries would be greater than the earnings of fully employed workers in low-wage industries.

### MONETARY AND COMMERCIAL POLICIES

It is one of the weaknesses of the program that it is not linked with a monetary policy and commercial policy. The Committee ended its work before such a program was finished. Some brief indications were, however, made.

As to commercial policy, the Committee emphasizes that Sweden's interest is to have an international, multilateral world trade that shall be as free as possible. Swedish trade policy must take this into account. Therefore, we should continue a low tariff policy and refrain as far as possible from restrictions. The size of the Swedish exchange reserve is a limiting factor, however, in any consistent attempt to maintain a very high level of employment if other countries do not have it. So Sweden must support an international policy to keep up employment everywhere. In the meantime, the Committee thinks that some temporary control over imports may be needed during the transition period.[1]

In 1945, when this program was prepared, most people thought that Sweden was well on the way to a depression or some kind of recession. But as so often happens, the economic development fooled all prophets. The expected post-war inflationary boom—which Mr. Myrdal and some of his colleagues regarded as a predecessor of a depression—proved unexpectedly long-lasting and intense. All through 1947 and 1948 there was a growing inflationary pressure, with wage increases and slowly rising prices. A rather strict price control was instituted, under which a large amount of goods was produced at a loss or with little profit. Therefore producers tended to expand the output of other goods less strictly regulated and on which they made relatively large profits. So the real question in Sweden from the summer of 1946 has become not to avoid recession but to reduce the inflationary pressure, that is, to prevent an increase in the aggregate volume of demand relative to supply. The absence of a real monetary program in the wide sense of the word has made itself felt.

In January, 1947, and in the following years the government presented an outline of an investment budget for the

---

[1] From the summer of 1946 to the end of 1947 Sweden's reserves of gold and foreign exchange fell from about $700,000,000 to about $150,000,000 as a result of a policy that has been much criticized.

whole economy. There are stipulated sums for each kind of investment, and an analysis as to whether an investment should be maintained or reduced within the year or perhaps increased.

Instead of restricting the volume of investment in 1946 and 1947, the authorities permitted it to increase, up to the end of the latter year. The consequent overemployment led to wage increases in 1947 well above what was compatible with general price stability. Evidently there is a real need of a program to counteract inflationary booms; it is equally necessary that it be worked out beforehand, as was done in the case of the anti-depression program. The problem was not seriously tackled until the latter part of 1947. It then proved difficult to restrict the labor force in the building industry quickly enough and to bring about a transition of workers to export and consumer industries. In a democracy it seems more difficult to carry out a policy against overemployment and inflation than to put an anti-depression policy into effect. The overemployment and lack of balance in the internal economy led to an enormous import surplus in 1946–47, whereby our gold and foreign exchange reserve was reduced to a minimum. Import restrictions were imposed. Under these circumstances the need for trade restrictions is strong, and it would be the case to an even greater extent if Sweden tried to maintain a high level of employment by means of an expansionist policy during a world economic depression. So it would seem that for us and for almost all other countries—they are in a similar position with regard to the foreign exchange reserve—it is possible to make use of any scheme for combating a depression only if there exists an international coordinated policy to maintain a high level of employment. Here the United States can make two large contributions: It can try to maintain employment at home, and it can support a program of international collaboration. Only then can the measures to maintain employment in other countries succeed, and only then can the development be prevented of a commercial policy undesirable from economic and political viewpoints alike.

# 5. Economic Stability and the Structure of Society

THIS SUBJECT IS SO ENORMOUS that it is impossible in a single chapter to do more than make a few observations. In the last half century the organization of society has been characterized by a growth of centralized organizations and control. In business we have—at least in Europe—more monopolistic organizations, more cartels, more large-scale enterprise, and more influential trade associations. In the labor market, trade unions and employers' organizations have become very powerful. In most countries there is an increasing amount of municipal and government enterprise, covering a much wider field than it did fifty years ago. Furthermore, government supervision of economic and social conditions, such as private monopoly prices, transportation rates, and working conditions, has been growing irrespective of the changes that have taken place since 1939.

It seems difficult not to believe that there has been a growing need for some such organization. Owing to the rising importance of fixed capital, as well as various rigidities on the labor market, the economic system does not adapt itself so easily to economic changes as it did in the nineteenth century. Economic depressions seem to have grown more serious, at least as far as employment conditions are concerned, and that also has called for expanded government action.

There is another reason why I think one can say that there has been a growing need for a firmer organization in the economic and social field, one reason which is not independent of the others, but which should be mentioned separately, namely, the different mental attitude of the twentieth century. In the nineteenth century "the merchant attitude" with its firm belief in free enterprise and free competition prevailed. In the twentieth century, this attitude has to some extent given way to "an engineer's mentality"—a belief in organization and a predilection for collaboration. In the social field, the risk of starvation has certainly become much smaller than it was fifty or a hundred years ago, but strangely enough, the feeling of insecurity seems to have grown stronger than it was in the earlier period. A gradual change of this sort has taken place, that has nothing to do with the other cause of insecurity—the international political tension and the risk of war. It is not unjustifiable to speak of a general "decline of optimism." People no longer believe, as they did quite generally a few decades ago, particularly in the United States, that next year will be much better than the present one, and the year after that the best we have ever experienced.

This more cautious attitude and the attendant feeling of insecurity has led to a popular demand for more organization both in the private and in the public field. While this change in attitude has been developing, the economic resources of society have been increasing. Governments have come into a position to provide for much better social security—chiefly by means of social insurance—than was possible heretofore.

MORE ABILITY TO CENTRALIZED CONTROL

At the same time, we have acquired a greater technical ability to make society subject to central regulation and control. The telephone, telegraph, the radio, newspapers, the new office techniques, the expanded statistics—all these make it possible to exercise a central direction, whether in the economic field, the military field, or elsewhere, which was quite unthinkable a century ago. In comparing tendencies in our society with mercantilist societies, which also experimented with central direction and control, we must not overlook this very fundamental difference between our times and earlier periods.

I find it impossible to avoid an impression that the process —most obvious in industrialized countries—which I have now very briefly outlined means to a large extent a double adaptation of the organization of society to new technical and psychological conditions. Changes in international conditions, the changing role and structure of international capital movement, and the obstacles to international migration have a more intimate connection with wars and the preparation for wars. Hence, they are not, as compared with the changes in the domestic organization of economic life, a rational and reasonable adaptation to new basic conditions.

### PROBLEM OF EMPLOYMENT MAINTENANCE

A few observations may be made on the calls for different forms of organization that arise from a wish to keep employment on a high and stable level. This problem is, of course, a very important one. Some economists lean towards the view— and I belong to them—that if Germany had not been hit by a severe unemployment crisis in the years 1930–32, it is quite probable that Hitler would never have come into power. The

Nazi vote went down from 1924 to 1928, while economic conditions were good, but started rising again when the depression set in.

So one might perhaps go so far as saying that if economic policy in Germany and elsewhere had been wiser, we might not have had to suffer a Second World War. No doubt, however, opinions like these are generally regarded as an expression of the megalomania of the economists—perhaps not entirely without reason.

Unfortunately, the problem of keeping the economic system —and, thereby, employment—on a stable level seems to become more and more difficult. I agree with Mr. Loveday, the former head of the League of Nations economic and financial section, that perhaps the main reason for this is the fact that the durable instruments play a growing role in modern society. I am thinking not only of machines and other instruments of production, but of the durable consumers' goods as well. Even if there should not in the future be a higher ratio of investment to national income than hitherto, yet the fact that a large and growing stock of capital instruments is in use and must be kept up through the production of new instruments to offset depreciation would be—as it is in our time—a cause of instability. Not only the new investment but the reinvestment as well may be partly put off for a year or two in a way which intensifies the economic fluctuations. Of course, the United States, which has the highest standard of living in the world, is the outstanding example of this. Nowhere do the durable consumers' goods play as large a role as here. Mr. D. H. Robertson of Cambridge has said once that the rise of the United States toward economic world leadership "looks like making life bumpier for the rest of us." I think there is something in that.

I have already advanced some views about the problem of how to make the employment and economic conditions in general more stable. Evidently, quite radical measures are called for if we are to hope for success. Above all large fluctuations in the volume of investment have to be prevented. To survey very briefly organized action in the domestic field by public authorities and other organizations, everybody agrees that it will not be easy to get public works started by governments and municipalities on a suitable scale *in time*. I have mentioned subsidies for housebuilding and for purchases of durable consumers' goods in depressions. There is also the cyclical balancing of the budget and various tax measures. Monopoly control will also be necessary to prevent costs from getting out of line in different industries.

It seems obvious that if we are to arrive at a relatively stable volume of investment there must be a close collaboration between private business and government. Some voluntary or involuntary adaptation of the volume of private investment is essential. A sound development of investment as a whole could be more easily achieved if business resorted to long-term planning of its own investments. The need for public control of private monopolies depends on the extent to which certain types of malicious monopolistic practices in business are avoided, as contrary to accepted behavior patterns.

As to the trade unions, a continued and considerable rise in average wage and price levels would almost certainly make employment stability impossible in the long run. Therefore, it is desirable that the average wage level should not rise more quickly than the corresponding increase in productivity of industry as a whole. If it does so, the commodity price level will also rise. Of course, if profits are unnecessarily large a redistribution between profits and wages may take place. But once that has been done, what I have said holds good.

Furthermore, we want as little as possible of vicious changes in sectional cost levels, say, the relation between cost in investment trades and the average income level in the economy as a whole, because if sudden and irrational changes occur in such relations, then the volume of investment is bound to fluctuate, even if governments and business firms have the best of intentions to the contrary. For this reason, it is very important that unions do not refuse to accept a reasonable number of apprentices or do not prevent any other adaptation of the skilled labor force to a growing need.

Even if all these conditions could be fulfilled it would not be enough. In the case of large labor conflicts in some industries, which mean a violent disturbance in themselves, it will obviously be impossible to maintain a stable employment in other industries. This is a separate problem which I shall not discuss here at all. The question of the maintenance of industrial peace is really a very prominent part of the problem of employment stabilization.

### PILLARS OF EMPLOYMENT STABILIZATION

In my opinion there are three main pillars of a policy of employment stabilization: To adapt the different types of real investment in such a way that the aggregate volume of investment does not fluctuate very much and is adapted to the willingness to save; to secure a wage policy of the type indicated; and to maintain industrial peace.

It will obviously be very difficult in a society of our type to obtain all this. When governments try to stimulate business in depressions, they may easily overdo it. To avoid getting into over-full employment it is necessary to restrict the expansionist measures early enough, a thing that might be politically even more difficult than to start the expansionist measures quickly enough. It is far from certain that the government in a democratic state—or in other states—will find it possible to check tendencies towards expansion while considerable unemployment still exists, because it will not be a popular thing to do. Thus, over-full employment may be caused. And if it lasts for more than a brief period, overemployment necessarily leads to a lot of regulation and control—to price control, rationing, control of international trade, and various other things.

As to business and business organization, it will probably not be easy to bring about a voluntary adaptation of investment. But it would probably be even more difficult to get a wage policy of the kind I have indicated, if we are to have the freedom on the labor market we have been used to and value so highly in most western European countries. What justification is there for the expectation that an individual labor union should not, during a time of very high employment, make attempts to utilize this favorable position to increase its wages, even if that should bring costs—for example in building—out of line with the average income level? If such demands are put forward and accepted, inflation is caused. If they are not accepted, there is of course a risk of labor conflicts. Such con-

flicts may come at inopportune moments, as they did in Sweden in 1933, when we were just about to start the expansion
of public investment to bring about recovery.

  Some people think that these difficulties are so formidable
that until we have all become much better educated than we
are and much more sensible, too, economic freedom will have
to be seriously restricted—assuming that we prefer that to having large fluctuations in price levels and employment. Most
Socialists accept an economic system with a very large expansion of control as a permanent thing. Many businessmen, on
the other hand, seem inclined to prefer the fluctuations rather
than to have even a small amount of central direction and
control. Personally, I consider both these attitudes unrealistic.
If an average of 88–90 percent employment and a freer economic system were preferred to 93–95 percent and some central direction, then I am convinced that we would not be able
to keep this relatively free economic system very long. In the
event of a serious depression, with very little done to forestall
it, public opinion would call for action and there would probably be a sudden use of rather severe restrictions and regulations. At least in some European countries there would be a
grave danger of measures of nationalization on a large scale.
People would undoubtedly say that private business "has had
its chance"; it has shown that it cannot maintain a reasonable
level of employment, and therefore another system should be
tried.

DIFFERENT TYPES OF SOCIETY

  The future of an economic system built on private owner-
ship, individual initiative, and the free choice of occupation

seems to me to depend in no small measure on a timely preparation of a policy of employment stabilization and on the result it will obtain.

Can we expect such a policy of employment stabilization as
outlined above to succeed in an economic system not radically
different from the present one in Western democracies? Is a
full employment policy compatible with free and unrestrained
trade unions, that are trying to get the maximum increase in
wages for their members—is it compatible with a society
where businessmen are free to try to strive for maximum profits without any social considerations?

It seems to me obvious that a full employment policy with
any chance of reasonable and politically necessary success immediately takes us outside the realm of a liberal society of the
late nineteenth century type. Only a more interventionistic
system can succeed. In a comparison and analysis of different
types of society that might adequately solve the employment
stabilization problem—while salvaging as much as possible of
the things I have mentioned—we can, therefore, leave out of
account altogether the so-called Manchester Liberal Economic
System.

What is the alternative? Dismissing the communistic state,
which is too far from the ideas prevalent in all democracies as
to the desirable type of society, there are of course several other
possibilities. Two of these are often analyzed. The first is a
centrally directed economic system with a great deal of nationalization and above all of permanent government controls. It
is a socialist type of society. Let us call it the semi-socialistic
system.

The other is a *social-liberal* society of the kind the Western world, and certainly the Scandinavian countries, has been more or less drifting into in the last decades. To compare very briefly this social-liberal "frame economy" with the semi-socialistic state, the difference is not—as has often been said— that planning is characteristic in the one type of society and not in the other. The relevant thing is not a distinction between a planned economy and an unplanned economy. Planning is absolutely necessary in every society. The businessman who does not plan will soon go out of business. It is not a question of planning or not planning: it is a question of who is to do the planning? Are we to have more or less of *central* planning, control and direction?

It is quite possible to have a great deal of government statistical work, of investment councils, tariff policy, and so a certain amount of central planning, without changing the fundamental characteristic of a free enterprise system built on competition. But in the semi-socialistic state we have a more detailed and complete central planning direction and control. Is the major part of the planning and control to be done in this way by central bodies or is it to be handled by decentralized agencies—above all the private firms—as in the social-liberal system?

Both these types of economic societies seek to maintain the freedom and movement of the workers and the freedom of action of the trade unions. But the social-liberal society, which I call "a frame economy," does oppose widespread nationalization, rigid and permanent price controls and other detailed methods of government regulation, relying instead on the free pricing system and on measures of the town and regional planning type, tariff policy, and so on.

The town plan is really typical for much of the intervention by the social-liberal society, because it lays down certain limits, a certain frame, within which the individual can move freely. An economic and social frame organized by society—largely by means of legislation—rather than detailed regulation is the characteristic of that type of society.

Most of the policy to mitigate economic fluctuations is fundamentally social-liberal, because it is based principally on maintaining the volume of aggregate demand, a sort of "global" control that is not detailed and direct regulation.

In the more socialistic type of society, on the other hand, government plays a larger and more direct role in running business and telling businessmen what to do, thus controlling economic life to a greater extent and in closer detail.

How do these two types of system compare from the point of view of an employment stabilization policy? It is hard to deny that the semi-socialist state has certain technical advantages above the liberal-social society. It is not unimportant that the socialist state directly controls a larger share of the total volume of investment. Secondly, I should say—and I am well aware of the fact that this is not a non-controversial statement—that the absolute freedom of trade unions and of labor movements would not last very long in the socialist state. Hence, it would perhaps be less difficult to make the labor unions accept certain patterns of behavior, for example, with regard to wage policy. Furthermore, it cannot be denied that under a controlled wage policy a rather high volume of employment (not what I call overemployment, but close to it) would be possible without serious increases in prices. The condition is price control and production regulation on a large scale. Without such controls prices are apt to rise even in highly competitive industries long before the full employment state is reached for industry as a whole.

Evidently, in some respects there are greater possibilities of maintaining a high and stable level of employment in semi-socialistic states. However, it seems to me (and this, again, is not a non-controversial statement) that these possibilities are obtained at the expense of a very essential freedom in the economic sphere both for business firms and workers. There is also a very serious risk for the freedom of the individual in other respects in a society with so pronounced a concentration of power. Besides, an economic system of this sort enables less use of important incentives like the economic gain motive and, therefore, leads to slower progress and lower living standards than a freer system.

## IMPORTANCE OF EDUCATION AND WAGE POLICY

This brings me to some observations on the possibilities in a social-liberal society of having nation-wide organizations on the labor market or on the commodity markets, without the risk of huge increases either in wages or in prices. One can, of course, always fall back on education and say that if only we were, all of us, better educated and more reasonable anything would be possible. It is tempting to assume that once everyone understood that inflation is not good for any large groups, then no responsible person would call for measures leading to inflation. However, that is not true. It may be possible to raise incomes in *one* group without causing very much inflation. It is tempting for each one of them to try this. But if wage policy and the fixing of farm prices are to such an extent coordinated that all the different groups face the problem of income determination and inflation at the same time, then none of them can say, "Well, if *our* group gets a little more, that does not matter as long as the others keep quiet."

That is one reason why in Sweden we are approaching a situation in which most of the trade unions have to negotiate collective agreements at the same time every year, well knowing that whatever increases they win the white collar workers will get very soon afterwards, and the farmers as well, through an agreement with the government on farm prices.

In a society with this setup, when all the different groups have to act at about the same time, they cannot forget how their own action will influence the actions of the other groups. The government will have to watch the procedure, government mediation in labor negotiations will be required, and some prices and wages in state employment will be fixed by the government after negotiation. Evidently, if things do not develop as desired, there is grave risk that a system of very considerable government interference will emerge, step by step.

As to sectional monopolistic wage policies, it is very difficult to see how they can be avoided, because one cannot demand greater altruism from the unions than from other groups. A moderating influence may be exercised if the freedom of the individual union is restricted, and some trade union council— not an outside organization—representing all the unions attains a certain authority over the policy of the individual unions in special cases. That is already the case in Sweden in certain respects. The central governing body of the trade union movement can end a strike even if the majority of the striking workers have voted for its continuance.

The Committee on Stabilization, appointed by the League of Nations, says that trade unions should "think and act in terms of economic activity as a whole, rather than in terms of their own craft or industry only." I think we can all sympathize with that. But one must ask: Do all groups of businessmen act and think in those terms?

It is true, though, that there are two fundamental differences between labor and commodity markets that should be emphasized. Nation-wide trade unions, like those on the European continent, have a monopoly over labor in that field, whereas competing businessmen in an industry do not. Even if they had the same mental attitude as some unions, they do not wield the same power to raise prices, as long as competition prevails. Besides, confronted by a monopoly in the form of a trust or cartel, the government is able to control prices. It is not too difficult to prevent at least the most important of the abuses of monopolistic power in business on a large scale. The difficulties are for obvious reasons much greater in the case of powerful trade unions pursuing a monopolistic wage policy. With the support of an educated public opinion, governments may, however, limit the possibilities on the part of the unions to apply special checks on the influx of labor to the high wage industry.

### ADAPTATION AND COORDINATION OF INVESTMENT

Let me turn now to the problem of an adaptation of the total volume of investment and the coordination of private and public investment in a social-liberal society. To obtain the desired stability is, of course, a very difficult task. Monetary policy has an important role to play. In a society without direct and detailed public control over important fields of investment, a variation of interest rates and open market operations to restrict or expand credit will be necessary. But voluntary organs of coordination can no doubt help. It should be possible in a boom to discourage manufacturing industries from a highly excessive investment. For experience demonstrates that it is often wise to wait. With the suitable apparatus of councils and secretariats, and with some general economic education, it should also be possible to bring about a certain amount of coordination of the private investment and the public investment. But monetary policy by central banks, a reasonable expansion of public investment in depressions and restriction in booms, must lay the foundation for a relative stability in the total volume of investment.

On the whole we find, I think, that to avoid a more detailed government regulation we must have—under conditions existing in Europe, at least—some general rules of behavior as to both investment policy and wage policy, and the pressure of public opinion to support them. If public opinion is educated, its pressure on the different groups may in many cases be decisive.

THE INTERNATIONAL FIELD

In the international field we do, of course, require many things that we do not have. For instance, international organizations that help to maintain certain standards of behavior by the various nations in commercial policy fall into this category. One of the great merits of the American proposal to form an International Trade Organization was that this is central to the plan and it is fortunate, indeed, that it has to some extent been maintained as a basis for this organization. It is hardly ever possible to tie the hands of people completely by set rules, but certain limits, certain rules, can be established as to what is normal behavior; and thereby policy can be affected to a great extent.

Organizations like those mentioned in Chapter 3 to handle a policy of buffer stocks are also needed, in addition to the International Bank, the Monetary Fund, the International Labor Office, the Forestry and Agriculture Organization, and others. The greatest problem for such institutions will probably not be to get a sufficient number of first-rate experts, although even that may be difficult in periods when every country needs its experts at home. Above all, the difficulty will probably lie in securing political backing for the necessary international measures and for domestic economic policies consistent with the maintenance of high employment in the world at large. On the other hand, if we get effective international organizations of the kind I have mentioned, they can lend authority to sound principles and thereby influence domestic policies. They can also "educate" the politicians and experts who are sent to conferences and committees.

The need of coordinated policy arises from the fact that all countries form a part of one economic world. I have already stated that I do not think we need "prosperity in all countries to have prosperity anywhere." But violent fluctuations in countries in close economic contact with the rest of the world cannot occur without hurting everybody. It is not so much the low level of income in some parts of the world as the violent fluctuations that would cause the damage in the more prosperous countries. It is for this reason particularly that we need an integration of national economic policies, for example, with regard to expansionary and restrictionary measures. A permanent institution that attempted to coordinate the employment policies and to avoid detrimental reactions on trade balances would be useful.

It is not justified to be altogether gloomy about the difficulties confronting this kind of policy. Let me also say something about the more cheerful prospect, if we succeed in maintaining a relatively high level of employment in a social-liberal society. It seems reasonable to assume that with security of employment, the sense of insecurity will diminish. Many of the policies on the labor market which are harmful for production because they reduce efficiency (for example, the unwillingness to help in the development of labor-saving methods of production) are caused by a feeling that there is not a sufficient amount of work, and that, therefore, one must "save" some of it and "divide" it carefully. The reasons for such policies would to a large extent disappear if confidence in a stable employment were created. It is quite possible that the policies of the trade unions would become much more progressive when fear of unemployment disappeared. It might prove much easier to obtain collaboration between the various groups in a firm or industry, with the aim to increase output. On the other hand, a feeling of insecurity may serve as a stimulus to individual efficiency. We all know instances of going from over-full to somewhat incomplete employment; business managers will tell you that they get higher efficiency, higher output per hour. Personally, I am inclined to think that these are chiefly short-run observations and refer to the more immediate effects of fluctuations in employment from an unhealthy overemployment to a more balanced situation. On the whole, I take the

optimistic view that most people will work about as well in a
society where they have security—without overemployment—
as in one where they have insecurity. One can, I think, go even
further and expect many of them to work better in the former
society than in the latter, provided that they have the stimulus
of higher economic rewards in compensation for greater and
better efforts. So even if a few percent of the people work less
in the absence of the strong incentive of insecurity, the loss will
only be a small one.

It is tempting to speculate on what will happen with
regard to business risks in a society where everyone has a
feeling that employment can be and will be maintained. Obviously certain business risks will be reduced; the risks of large
losses will decline. The need for monopolistic agreements to
prevent "cut-throat competition" will be much reduced. It is
conceivable that new types of organization, new types of business firms, and new forms of financing might be found practicable under those conditions. If in the future the savings of the
rich play a smaller role than they have done up to the Second
World War, it will be necessary to utilize the savings of the
large masses of people for the financing of production and
trade even in what is now considered highly risk-carrying lines.

## PROBLEM OF ECONOMIC FREEDOM

Is it reasonable to hope that employment stabilization can
be achieved in a society that maintains economic freedom of
the type I have mentioned? The French statesman Clemen-
ceau once said that the essence of liberty is self-discipline, and
I think there is a great deal of truth in that. There are many
restrictions on our liberty in modern society which we do not

feel at all. Up to a certain point it is true that if we change our attitude as to what kind of restrictions are reasonable, we may cease to regard them as something that reduces our essential liberty.

Nevertheless, there are certainly great risks for liberty in a society that aims at employment stabilization on a high level. The very same factors that make central direction and control possible increase the possibilities of restricting individual liberty. In earlier centuries it was only to a minor extent possible to control what people were saying; but in the last war surveillance over telephone conversations revealed to governments what a lot of people were saying, including things that were meant only for private ears. So I do not think that one should talk lightly about the risks that are caused by growing possibilities of controlling the actions of individuals, possibilities that might lead governments and other bodies into temptation.

However, in spite of the risks, there is—also for people who want to defend liberty—a very preponderant argument in favor of an attempt to achieve employment stabilization on a reasonable level. If we do not succeed in preventing large-scale unemployment, or if we do get into long spells of over-full employment, then a strictly regulated economy will follow. That would be an even greater menace to liberty. The conclusion that long depressions would lead to a system of regulation that threatens liberty is tragic in a way, because it means that people will prefer serious restrictions on liberty rather than suffer insecurity and hardships. But I think that is the truth, and it would be fatal to overlook the consequences. Some liberals of the Manchester type, who in practice want a return to the economic system of the period before 1914, have failed to appreciate this fact.

## EMPLOYMENT POLICY AND PEACE

A relatively high level of employment will have important repercussions on international relations, not only in economic respects. Mr. Loveday, whom I have quoted once before, said ten years ago that "depressions, through the misery they create, through the mystery of their cause, through the fatalism and the antagonisms to which they give rise, are the gravest social danger and the greatest danger to peace and collective sanity and security to which the modern world is subject." I think it is obvious that nationalistic currents of thought are intensified during periods of depression. We need only look at the 1930s to find corroboration for this. If serious depressions are avoided, it will be much more difficult for nationalists to make propaganda not only against foreign goods but also against foreigners and foreign countries in general. The mental attitudes that develop under crisis conditions may be a danger to peace. Hence, sound economic conditions that reduce the need of "tariff wars" and similar kinds of measures are essential for any policy to preserve peace.

The reverse relation between peace and employment is still more obvious. If people start throwing atomic bombs at each other it will be too much to ask for employment stabilization.

These brief remarks on a large and important subject are of course not meant to be anything like an answer to the problems I have raised. Our system of society seems to be on trial with regard to its ability to solve the problems under discussion. There are other types of society in the world today which seem to me, personally, to offer less freedom and opportunity to individuals, but perhaps more security in other respects. This is a challenge to all of us, to all of those who want to defend a system of individual liberty, to help to work out solutions of these problems, and to see to it that those solutions are tried out in practice. I feel certain that only in a society which provides a reasonable degree of economic stability and security will liberty be maintained.

# 6. The Swedish Theory of Unused Resources

IT IS IMPOSSIBLE in a single chapter to summarize any theory about unused resources, but I shall try to present those parts of the Swedish theory which seem to be most relevant for economic policy.

It may be worth while to make the distinction between those changes in the employment of labor and other resources that are connected with variations in the aggregate demand for goods and services in terms of money, and those other changes in employment which may occur even if the aggregate demand for goods and services does not change.[1] It is true that this distinction is made only for the purpose of presentation and that in concrete cases no sharp cleavage is possible. In the 1920s, the changes in employment connected with variations in the total demand for goods and services were less frequently analyzed than the changes divorced from these variations. After the depression of the 1930s, however, special attention had to be given to them.

## WICKSELL'S THEORY

In Sweden the study of this problem had a natural starting point: the theory developed by Knut Wicksell. Wicksell was a peculiar man; he often put to himself questions which most people thought a little naive. This was the reaction in many

[1]The term "aggregate demand" is here used in the sense of aggregate "purchases." In other connections the word demand is used in the sense of "demand schedule."

quarters in Scandinavia when Wicksell formulated the question: "If the price of an individual commodity will go up when demand rises relative to supply, why should not the same thing be true if we take all commodities together? Why should not the same reasoning hold for the price of *aggregate* supply, and, thus, be applicable to changes in the general price level?"[2] It is true, we have been told by J. B. Say, the French economist, that this is not so, but maybe Say was wrong. Let us attempt, therefore, to follow this road, said Wicksell. How can total demand and purchases rise under given conditions of supply? He found that if people purchase capital goods or other goods for inventory, that is, if they spend for *investment purposes*[3] greater sums of money than correspond to the amounts other people want to save, then, to put it crudely, part of that investment will be financed not out of savings but out of "new purchasing power." The aggregate volume of demand will increase if "investment exceeds savings." Wicksell stressed very emphatically what Keynes later on discovered: that those who decide to save are not as a rule the ones who decide to invest. Therefore, there is no obvious reason why the two different groups should decide to invest and decide to save exactly the same amount. It is true that the rate of interest can exercise an equilibrating influence. But it was easy to show that the rate of interest cannot be relied upon "to equalize savings and in-

[2]See Knut Wicksell, "The Monetary Problem of the Scandinavian Countries," *Ekonomisk Tidskrift,* 1926 (reprinted in the English edition of Wicksell's well-known book *Interest and Prices,* London, 1936).

[3]"For investment purposes" here refers exclusively to purchases of new goods and services; the alternative is "for consumption purposes." Financial investment through the purchase of old assets—real estate, shares, bonds, etc.—is quite another matter.

vestments." And so Wicksell came to concentrate his attention on what happens when "savings differ from investments." To explain this, an account of a time-using process is required. Wicksell, therefore, developed his now well-known theory of *a cumulative process of inflation*. His pupil, Professor Erik Lindahl, who completed and revised Wicksell's work,[4] directed attention to changes in the demand for consumers' goods, a subject which had held a secondary place in Wicksell's analysis. Before the depression in the thirties Lindahl had analyzed the effects of various kinds of economic policies on both the aggregate supply and demand for consumers' goods and on investment.

### THE UNEMPLOYMENT REPORTS

In 1931, when the world economic depression had begun, the Swedish Unemployment Commission asked a number of economists to write reports on what would happen if different kinds of economic policy were used to combat unemployment. These reports were published in the years 1933 to 1935.[5]

It became evident that there were certain theoretical problems that had to be cleared up. Obviously, output and investment can be expanded during a process of a recovery from a depression, even though savings are very small in the depressed state. There seems to be no primary increase in savings. The

[4]See Erik Lindahl, *The Means of Monetary Policy* (in Swedish), Stockholm, 1930, and *Studies in the Theory of Money and Capital*, London, 1939.

[5]Besides the works by Johanson and myself that are mentioned below, see Gunnar Myrdal, *The Economic Effects of Financial Policy*, Stockholm, 1933, and Dag Hammarskjöld, *The Spread of Trade Variations*, Stockholm, 1933 (both in Swedish).

increase takes place in investment. How can investment rise when savers do not decide to save more? What is meant by saying that investment exceeds savings? After all, one cannot get capital goods out of nothing. One cannot make machines with banknotes. Investment requires saving. Where then do the new and increased savings come from?

The answer was found through an analysis of the Wicksellian cumulative process, by using Professor Myrdal's convenient distinction between forward-looking and backward-looking, between an analysis *ex ante*—looking forward—and *ex post*—looking backward. One can consider a period that is going to begin in the future or just now, or one can look back upon a period that is already finished. There is a need of a concept of income *ex ante*—expected income—and one *ex post*—realized income; similarly with savings: planned savings and realized savings, and so on.

To explain a process, the attendant circumstances must first be recorded with the aid of a period analysis. One can date the events conveniently by saying this happened in that period and that happened in another period. By this kind of bookkeeping, the sequence of events can be followed, taking into account the time lags between the various reactions, whenever necessary.

At the end of any period, it is possible to note what has occurred to summarize certain transactions, and to "close the accounts," so to speak. It is possible to ascertain what the incomes, the investments, and the savings have been during the period. This is an account *ex post*.

However, such an account provides no explanation. An explanation must run in terms of factors that govern actions; and actions refer to the future. Therefore, one must analyze expectations and plans for the future. An analysis *ex ante* is required.

The expectations and plans are to some extent based on the experiences of the earlier periods, but they are not, as a rule, related to experience in a mechanical way. It is true that contracts often carry over from one period to another, as also the supply of productive resources. To that extent there are formal and mechanical or physical connections. However, there are also psychological connections of a different nature. For instance, why do people plan to increase their purchases of consumer goods above the amount spent the preceding period? Usually, because something has led them to expect larger incomes. Why do they plan to increase investment? As a rule, because some events in the recent past have brightened the chances for future profit.

Evidently, in this forward-looking analysis, we have the same categories as in a backward-looking analysis. We have expected incomes as well as realized incomes. We have planned investment, planned savings, and so on, just as we have realized incomes and realized savings in the backward-looking analysis.

### THE CAUSAL ANALYSIS

To explain what happens, a combination of the *ex post* and the *ex ante* analysis is necessary. We have to survey the events during a period and then compare what actually happened with what was expected to happen. Thereafter, we study how new expectations and plans are formed on the basis of the earlier discrepancies between plans and the actual course of events, taking into account new outside events.

It is unnecessary to go into the somewhat subtle questions of definitions of the basic concepts. One thing, however, should be mentioned. When we look backward to see what has happened during a period, it seems most practical to define income in such a way that the volume of savings is—always—equal to the volume of new investment in terms of money values.[6] This is a matter of convenience. Many people have preferred other definitions, but to me one consideration always seems decisive. If I ask where did all the new real capital, the new buildings, machines, et cetera, come from that have been produced during a finished period, it seems to me natural to say the following: As these things have been produced, they have been part of income; they have not been consumed, because they are still there; so they all correspond to a part of income which has been saved. Therefore, the most natural thing is to define the basic concepts in such a way that when you look backwards, savings agree with investment. On the other hand, *planned* savings and *planned* investment need not, of course, be equal; one group may plan to buy more goods than another group plans to sell. Behind this whole intricate discussion of discrepancies between planned savings and planned investment lies this simple fact: When the sum of all planned purchases differs from the sum of all planned sales, then there exists the very same discrepancy as that which has been more commonly expressed by saying that planned savings differ from planned investment. A process of expansion or contraction is inevitable.

### THE SOURCES OF INCREASED SAVINGS

After this brief indication of the character of the theoretical reasoning, let us return to the question, Where do the savings

[6] Cf. my book (in Swedish) on *Monetary Policy, Public Works, Subsidies and Tariffs as Remedies for Unemployment*, Stockholm, 1934, and "The Stockholm Theory of Saving and Investment," *The Economic Journal*, 1937.

come from when the volume investment is increased in a period of recovery from a depression? Let us assume that investment is stepped up but that nobody plans to increase savings—so far. What will happen? Obviously, the total sales will rise; more goods will be produced; wage earnings will rise also, even though, at the start, wage rates may be assumed to be constant. Wage earners will save more money or will spend less of the money they have already saved. To spend such money or buy on credit is a negative saving, which is now reduced. Evidently, the aggregate savings of wage earners will be increased. Furthermore, producers making unexpectedly large profits will save more than they had expected to save. At the end of a period, it is seen that incomes have exceeded expected incomes and that, therefore, savings have exceeded planned savings. In brief, total savings rise above planned savings in both groups. This, however, is not the only force that makes for agreement between savings and the increased volume of investment. The total volume of new investment will in some cases fall short of what people planned; for example, commodity stocks will have been reduced. In other words, there has been an unintentional disinvestment, a negative investment through reduction of commodity stocks. That "offsets" some of the output of new capital goods. So even though people may have built the houses and the machinery that they planned to build, yet the total addition to real capital will be found to have been smaller than was expected. The agreement between realized investment and realized savings has been brought about in that way, too. The net investment has been smaller than the planned new investment.

Many may feel that all this talk in quantitatively precise terms of "planned savings" and "planned investment" and so on is rather artificial. That may be so, but consider by way of comparison the Marshallian supply and demand curves. I suppose all economists have been brought up on that analysis, and few of us could do without it. Now, the Marshallian demand curves assume that we know how much butter we would buy if the price were so high or so high or so high. Yet if we actually asked ourselves how much we would buy at double the current price, few of us would know. In the theory it is necessary to assume a certain quantitative precision instead of vague ideas. Otherwise, a theoretical tool of great practical usefulness would not be at our disposal.

Personally, I do not think that a cautious use of either the Marshallian curves or the *ex ante* concepts does any essential violence to reality. It is, of course, desirable that as many of our concepts as possible should be related to the statistical material. Professor Allyn Young of Harvard University said twenty-four years ago that the subject matter of pricing theory is in the form of statistical time series, while almost none of the theoretical concepts are such as can be related to these series. However, in this case, with regard to savings and investment, we are not quite so badly off as we are with regard to the supply and demand analysis. One can get statistics about investment plans. For many years we have had in Sweden figures for the planned investments covering about two-thirds of the manufacturing industries; and, of course, when government subsidies influence housebuilding so strongly, it should be easy to ask government authorities for their plans. That would help somewhat. On the other hand, at the end of a year of over-full employment one finds that investment plans were not realized. In the first place, some buildings that were planned were not built. Moreover, producers of building materials have reduced their stocks. In other words, there has been a disinvestment, an unintentional reduction of inventories of building materials owing to unexpectedly large purchases by constructors. It is not at all inconceivable that in the future we will be able to get selective statistics about such things.

It is worse, I admit, in the case of savings, because it is very difficult to gather any statistics about planned savings. However, with the concepts mentioned above as a starting point, considerable progress can be made by studying the changes in the purchases for consumption goods and the changes in the purchases for investment purposes and by analyzing the causal factors behind the decisions of individual firms or persons; and this can be done without summing up "psychological" quantities such as planned savings for the country as a whole.

What we are driving at in the analysis of processes of expansion and contraction is really rather simple. Expansion means that total purchases are increased from one period to another. There is a rise in the volume of goods produced, in prices, or in both. How can purchases be made to rise? Remember that purchases are either made for consumption or for investment. Let us consider the question, What makes consumers' demand rise? The answer is either a decision to save less or an expectation of higher income. If people expect higher incomes, they may buy more consumers' goods, even though they do not decide to save less.

On condition that there is not by mere chance a fall in the investment demand which offsets or more than offsets the rise in the total demand for consumption, the outcome will be an increase in the aggregate demand. In the same way, if a decision to save less is not offset by a decision to invest less, then there is an increase in the aggregate purchases. One can state the formula thus: planned investment exceeds planned savings. But one can also express it in the terms I have used immediately above, which is perhaps more straightforward. For the concentration of attention on the discrepancy between planned saving and planned investment is apt to leave out of account the possibility that people may expect higher incomes and therefore may buy more goods for consumption, even if they do not decide to save less, and if investment is unchanged. If so, there will be a process of expansion, even if planned saving equals planned investment—which is quite possible.

But why should people expect higher incomes in a future period? Many answers are possible. The most obvious is that wage rates may have been increased on the first of January, and therefore the expectation of higher incomes during the following month may induce more buying in the first week of January. Or businessmen, when closing their accounts, may find that their profits were higher in December or in the last quarter of the year than anticipated. If sales curves are rising they may expect to make still larger profits in the coming year and may feel that they can now buy for their wives the fur coats they could not afford last year. So it is not at all an unrealistic assumption that when people expect higher incomes they therefore buy more, even though they do not decide to save less. This is all rather simple, at least to minds that have not been misled by too much study of conventional monetary theory of the quantity theory type.

## THE SPEED OF THE REACTIONS

The essence of the matter is this: how do consumption purchases and investment purchases vary from one period to another? In order to explain that, one must study plans and expectations and their relations to what has actually happened in the earlier period. In order to be able to describe and explain the effects of an increase in investment, it is—as I have mentioned above—necessary to take into account the speed of the reactions, because the reactions often go in different directions, and the outcome depends on "what happens first."

Let us assume that house rents are increased 10 percent. How quickly will houseowners increase their purchases? And how quickly and how much will the people who pay the higher rents reduce their purchases of consumption goods? In other words, to what extent will savings be reduced by the tenants and increased by the houseowners? I think that the effect on production and prices will depend on the relative speed of these reactions. If houseowners are very quick to step up their demands while others are reluctant to reduce their purchases, the outcome may be that the price of other commodities will rise. The average price level is then increased not only because rents are higher but because other goods have also gone up. But if houseowners are slow to increase spending while other consumers are quick to reduce it, the result will be a tendency for the prices of other goods to fall, and this may offset the increase in the house rents. If costs of living go up, how speedily will wage rates be affected? That is obviously another question to be considered.

If the wheat crop promises to be large, the price of wheat may fall even before the crop comes on the market. Prices may fall so much that farmers expect lower incomes and reduce their purchases accordingly. It may be that the price of wheat flour and bread has not been reduced as yet. Sometimes an interval passes before bakers reduce the price of bread. The consumers do not benefit by the lower wheat prices at once. There may be no over-all increase in consumer purchases, but there will be a reduction in purchases by farmers. Besides, if industries producing farm machinery experience a drop in demand, they may reduce their investment purchases, and this also may cause some unemployment.

### SAVINGS AND INTEREST RATES

What will be the effect of an increase in savings in a balanced economic situation, for instance, of a decision to put more money in the banks? According to the orthodox theory, the rate of interest will fall and investment will grow. But this is far from certain. If savings grow, a decline in the demand for consumers' goods takes place. Other things being equal, that will cause reduced profits and losses; businessmen will sell less consumers' goods and more goods will be left on their shelves. They will, therefore, need more credit to finance their business; so they will turn to the banks and may ask for just as much new credit as other people have put into the banks! If so, there will be no more money in the banks; there will be no direct reason for changing the interest rates or the lending policy on the part of the banks. The net effect of the decision to save more would be a tendency towards a depression but not a lower interest level, until the depression has had an indirect influence in that direction.

However, I do not think that either of these two explanations—the orthodox and the newer one—can be generally correct. As a matter of fact, as already indicated, everything depends on the speed of the reactions. If people who save money put it in savings accounts, and if businessmen instead of borrowing from the banks draw on their checking accounts— when business declines they need less cash—it is quite possible that the monetary authorities, watching the development in the banks, will draw such conclusions that the rates of interest are lowered. Besides, bankers, even without any change in the rates of interest, seeing that the deposits in savings accounts grow, will feel that they are in a position to lend more money for certain investment projects, where earlier they have been rather reluctant to do so. This rise in investment may compensate for the decline in consumers' demand. Hence, it is not certain that a fall in the aggregate demand will take place. I must add, however, that I do not find it probable that as a rule a sufficiently quick increase in the grant of credit will be called forth to prevent such a fall completely. But it *may* happen. Thus, no general explanation of the effects of increased savings is possible.

I often feel inclined to refer to a little incident during a discussion at the Economic Club in London. Someone was making rather bold, brief, and determined statements. Old Alfred Marshall grew impatient with the cocksureness of the speaker, and when a more than usually emphatic remark was made, Marshall called out from one of the benches, "All short statements are wrong." Whereupon another member of the club added, "Isn't that one?"

## THE DETERMINATION OF THE RATE OF INTEREST

What I have just said about savings brings me to the question of what forces govern the changes in the rate of interest. The basic assumption with regard to interest that we used in the Swedish analysis of unused resources was a simple one: Within certain limits the level of interest rates can be arbitrarily fixed by the monetary authorities. I think that, given certain conditions with regard to the foreign exchange position, this is on the whole a justified assumption.

Why can the monetary authorities fix the level of interest rates at will? Because interest rates depend on the supply of and demand for credit, and the monetary authorities can increase or reduce the supply of credit of different sorts. A change in savings does not—as we have seen—necessarily and directly lead to a change in the supply of credit. Does this mean that the rate of interest has no relation to the volume of savings? Of course not, but the connection between the rate of interest and the willingness to save and the supply of credit is an indirect one.

Let us assume certain income and profit expectations and certain plans to consume and save. The existing rate of interest will then determine the volume of investment plans. In any case, changes in interest rates will cause variations in the volume of investment. If in a stable economic situation the interest level is considerably reduced, investment purchases will grow. As a consequence, production will expand or prices will rise or commodity stocks will be reduced. Possibly two, or all three, of these things will happen. Obviously, other things being equal, the height of the rate of interest governs the economic development, because it influences the volume of investment—possibly also the will to save—and thereby the movement of aggregate purchases.

If a certain economic development is called "normal" (for example a stable retail price level), then there may be a certain level of interest rates, perhaps several combinations of interest rates, that correspond to or are compatible with this normal economic development. In some cases no such interest level exists, as in a very deep depression when many unfavorable factors influence business.

Take a situation where there is a "normal" development and interest level. A higher interest level would give less investment and a tendency towards recession. Lower interest rates would bring about a tendency towards expansion. However, if people increased their willingness to save, a greater volume of investment and a lower rate of interest would be compatible with this normal economic development, for instance a stable price level. On the other hand, if people reduced their willingness to save, only a smaller volume of investment and a higher interest level would be compatible with this normal economic development. Thus, the central idea in orthodox interest theory, that *savings and investment govern interest rates,* seems to me to be essentially true. But the connection between interest rates and savings and investment is not that of a market where you have two supply and demand curves for savings and investment respectively. There is no market for savings; there is only a market for credit, or rather several markets for credit of different sorts. The connection between savings and investment, on the one hand, and the rate of interest, on the other hand, is indirect and goes chiefly via the influence of the rate of interest on the volume of investment and the consequent effect on the size of income and savings, given a certain propensity to save. The amount of credit that is supplied can be varied at will by the banking system and, thus, within limits, the interest rates can be governed. But the height of the interest level and the volume of investment activity that can exist, if we want a certain economic development, depends on the propensity to save.[7]

I shall come back to this question again in the next lecture, because this is one point that I feel has been oversimplified by the Keynesian theory.

It is of course rather arbitrary to call any special economic development normal; hence, the designation of any particular interest level as normal is also arbitrary. In a changing world that is never in equilibrium, there can be no specific "equilibrium rate of interest."

If one looks upon this theoretical analysis of changes in output and interest rates as an amplification of the business cycle theory of the 1920s, it is not in any way revolutionary or startling. It puts in more precise terms—and that is, of course, not unimportant—a common sense view about the rise of investment in a recovery, about the flexible dependence of interest rates on savings and investment, and so on. The observation that changes in investment activity have a central role in business fluctuations has been stressed in practically every study

[7]A fuller discussion of this problem is to be found in my book on *Monetary Policy, Public Works, Subsidies and Tariffs as Remedies for Unemployment* (in Swedish), Stockholm, 1934.

of business cycles in the last four decades. It has also long been common knowledge that one can improve business conditions through public works. With the theoretical reasoning above one can explain the problems more clearly, but the conclusions are not so different that any condemnation of earlier theories is justified. The Swedish theory made it possible to analyze changes in employment with, I think, less violent simplifications than those used in Keynes's general theory. The startling results of the latter theory, which has been regarded in many quarters as quite revolutionary, seems due either to these simplifications or to specific assumptions about a durable tendency to "oversaving," "underinvestment," and "underemployment." (See next chapter.)

THE INADEQUACY OF THE QUANTITY THEORY

The Swedish approach—which, by the way, is in several ways similar to the one used by R. G. Hawtry and D. H. Robertson and which must have been influenced by their analysis—differs considerably from the old quantity theory of money. I think one can distinguish between two approaches to monetary theory. One approach is through a study of the movements of the money units. How fast do they move? What is their velocity? What happens to the quantity of money? What is the construction of the banking system, which affects the velocity of money, and so on? That is the method where the observer hangs himself on to the money units, so to speak, follows them and sees what happens. That is the quantity theory approach.

The other method starts from the fact that everything depends on the actions of individuals, businessmen as well as consumers. When and why and how much do their income and profit expectations change? Why do they decide to vary their purchases for consumption and for investment? What is the time lag between different events? The speed of the psychological reactions has very little connection with any speed in the movement of the money units. Changes in the quantity and velocity of money, therefore, are relatively uninteresting for a study of the processes of expansion or contraction, except in one respect, namely, with regard to their influence on the rate of interest and the willingness of the banks to lend.

### CHANGES IN THE QUANTITY OF MONEY

I think one could concentrate most of what is important in the study of the banking mechanism on that very question: How are the rates of interest and the credit policy of banks affected? The supply of money adapts itself to the need of the "circulation" and has little direct influence, except to the extent it affects interest rates and banking policy. The economic history of the last two decades gives numerous examples of countries where the quantity of money has been doubled, without any other consequence than a drop in the interest level, an important fact in itself, no doubt. One can find other periods of, say, three to four years when the quantity of money has been increased by 50 percent and yet no fall in the rate of interest has taken place. If so, the fact that people have a little more money in cash or in checking accounts, and perhaps less money in savings accounts, really does not much affect their decisions as to consumption and investment. For instance, if in order to finance certain expenditures the state should borrow from the central bank instead of from the money market, this will influence the quantity of money in circulation. But unless it also changes the rates of interest and credit conditions, it will not, I think, affect the volume of purchases. These purchases depend chiefly on income expectations and profit expectations, and the public does not vary its opinion in these respects because there is a change in the quantity of money.

It is true that purchases of commodities depend not only on the *willingness* to buy but also on the *ability* to buy. Thus, unless you can get credit, you have to have cash. Cash and credit conditions, therefore, set a limit for purchases for any one individual during a certain period; but inside those limits, spending depends on willingness to buy, which is governed by income expectations and the propensities to consume and save.

It will be found, I think, that in most cases changes in the willingness to buy are the decisive factor, because few people buy to the very limit of what they could buy. The important thing is how they vary their purchases within the limits of what they could buy, and that has often very little to do with the quantity of money. Hence, it is not the speed with which the money transfers are made from one person to another, increasing the cash of the latter, but rather the speed of the psychological reactions with regard to income and profit expectations that governs the changes in purchases, prices, and production.

### WAGE CHANGES AND UNEMPLOYMENT

It would carry me too far to attempt to analyze here the relation between wage changes and the volume of employment as developed in the Swedish studies in the early thirties.[8] But

[8]See particularly Alf Johanson, *The Wage Development and Unemployment,* Stockholm, 1934.

the central idea is quite simple. The volume of employment is equal to the sums paid out in wages divided by the average earnings per worker. That is a truism. If you want to increase employment you must either increase the demand for labor in terms of money or reduce wage rates or both. An increase in the total sum of purchases of goods and services (and therefore, indirectly, in the demand for labor) for instance, through increased government expenditures in a depression will, as a rule, increase employment, for it is unlikely that it would cause a proportional or more than proportional rise in wage rates. It is much more difficult to say anything about the effects of primary changes in wage rates. For wages enter both as costs and as income in the economic system. If you reduce wage costs and purchases by the same amount, say, by $100,000,000, employment need not be directly affected—on condition that prices are lowered as much as costs. Let us disregard savings for the moment. Then people will be able to buy the same quantity of goods and there will be no direct change in employment. Much depends, of course, on how wage changes affect profit expectations and, in that way, investment purchases. A decline in wages may lead to a rise in investment: then employment will probably rise also. It is impossible here to generalize, for the reaction of investment will depend on the special conditions which exist when the wage alteration is made. If the public is led to expect a further decline in prices, the wage reduction may lead to a drop in investment. But if the belief prevails that costs have now reached rock bottom, there will probably be an increase in investment. Of course, one cannot leave out of account what happens to savings. Besides, the process will be different when prices are not immediately reduced as much as costs.

It is important, I think, to stress that if aggregate demand in terms of money is maintained—which is possible to achieve by such special measures as government purchases and public works—a reduction in wage rates will lead to an increase in employment. This is no recommendation as to policy—far from it—but the statement of a fact.

### RELATIVE WAGE RATES

As investment demand is so important, special attention must be given to the relation between wage rates in the investment trades, for instance, in construction, and wage rates in the consumers' goods industries. (Cf. Chapter 2.) Other things being equal, a *relative* cheapening of labor or other cost reductions in the investment industries will tend to revive investment.

If house rents go down, relative to income, for instance, if they rise less than income, people can afford larger dwellings. So it is much more likely that a wage reduction in the investment trade will increase employment than that wage reduction in the consumers' goods industries will do so. A relative change in these wage rates can exercise an influence on investment similar to the effect of a change in the rate of interest!

Perhaps the most reliable method of increasing employment in a depression would be to expand the aggregate demand while keeping the price of labor stable. For then more labor can find employment. Thus government expenditure, financed by borrowing in a way that does not reduce private borrowing and investment, plays an important part in an anti-depression policy. Another way is to create conditions favorable for a revival in private investment. A feeling among employers that the general wage level will not fall can help to bring about this effect.

## INFLUENCE OF INTERNATIONAL TRADE

So far I have said nothing about the influence of international trade. It is fairly obvious that the economy of a country is affected by an increase in the foreign demand for its exports. The consequence is an expansion of the domestic purchases. The expansionist tendency of the increased foreign demand exhausts its effects when the rise in export values is offset by increased imports. As long as exports rise more than imports, the consequent export surplus is a new investment abroad. Its direct effects are similar to those of increased investment at home. However, if bilateral trade agreements are made, whereby exports and imports are simultaneously increased above a formerly restricted volume, then there is no investment abroad. The effect on the domestic economy is similar to that caused by a rise in consumption demand accompanied by a rise in production, while savings and investment remain unchanged. No "multiplicatory" effects appear. In some cases, however, domestic investment will rise as a result of the increase in foreign trade.

Changes in wage rates and other cost items, as well as in efficiency, can of course influence the volume of imports and exports and thereby the total development of output and employment in the way indicated.

SOME LABOR MARKET PROBLEMS

So far I have discussed exclusively the first of the two questions mentioned by way of introduction, namely, the relation between changes in the volume of aggregate demand in terms of money, on the one hand, and the volume of employment, on the other hand. But this is really only half the story. I shall be very brief about the second part, which is less controversial.

The average number of unemployed persons in a certain period is governed by the number of workers that are unemployed at the beginning plus those who are dismissed or who end their jobs of their own will, plus the number of new persons entering the labor market—all those who are looking for jobs—multiplied by the average period of waiting before they find a job. It is obvious, therefore, that, other things being equal, unemployment can be reduced by improved organization of the labor market, for example a more effective labor exchange system, as well as increased mobility of labor between places and occupations. But the mobility of labor, which is helpful, must be distinguished from the erratic movements of workers who leave a job for the sake of change only, and thus cause an increase in unemployment for brief periods of time.

Another well-known consideration is the following: If wages are not adapted to the quality of labor, but if a full wage is requested for laborers who offer a lower quality of work, these workers may be unemployed permanently, or will find jobs only when business is good.

## MONOPOLISTIC WAGE POLICY AND EMPLOYMENT

I think all this is obvious. It can be said of another kind of unemployment also which, however, in recent years has not been much studied. I am thinking about the influence of monopolistic wage and price policies under conditions of incomplete mobility of labor. *If the size and character of demand for goods and services is fixed in terms of money* then only a certain quantity of a certain productive factor—for instance, labor—will be demanded at a certain price. The higher the price of that factor, the smaller the employment of it. As a matter of fact, a wage increase can bring about a fall in aggregate purchases. Thus, if the wages of a certain quality of labor are substantially raised, then its employment will tend to fall, because there will be a tendency to use relatively less of that labor and more of other factors, and it may fall also because the decline in the quantity of total output will tend to reduce the aggregate demand for all productive factors. However, if other conditions making for an expansion of demand are at work at the same time, it is possible that the volume of aggregate demand will not fall. It may even rise. Nevertheless, there remains a *tendency* to a decline in the demand for the factor of which the price has been raised.

Were workers to move easily from a high-wage industry where wages have been raised, to other occupations with lower wage levels and if these wage levels can be somewhat reduced, then an increase in unemployment can perhaps be avoided, or only a very brief increase in unemployment occur. But if the number of workers seeking employment in the high-wage industries—where wages have gone up—does not fall sufficiently, that is, does not increase elsewhere, and if the wage levels elsewhere are not flexible, then unemployment will be created by the original rise in wages. It is true, of course, that an economic expansion caused by quite different conditions may prevent this from happening. But the tendency toward a fall in employment will nevertheless be there. A relative rise in the wage level in capital goods industries may have a direct detrimental influence on the volume of investment, as I have already mentioned.

In the reasoning above, I have, however, ignored the possibility that wage increases may make new investment profitable and may therefore lead to increased employment. But besides such tendencies, which cause changes in aggregate demand, there is always a tendency toward a smaller demand for a factor that has been made relatively expensive to use. So a monopolistic trade union policy will in itself have a tendency to reduce employment for those types and qualities of labor.

MONOPOLISTIC PRICE POLICY

A similar effect on employment may of course be called forth by monopoly prices on certain commodities. Monopolistic price policy will reduce demand for the productive factors used and will set up a need for an adaptation in the corresponding industries, as in the cases above, if unemployment is to be avoided. There is, however, one difference: Because the labor in these occupations has not become more expensive, there will be no tendency to substitute other factors for the labor factor. Besides, there may be less unwillingness on the part of workers to move to other occupations, since the wage level in the old one has not been increased.

On the other hand, the part of the increased profits of the monopolistic firms likely to be saved is larger than the part saved from increased wages in the former case. This in itself may cause a tendency towards a contraction and a fall in employment, unless there is some other force making for increased investment. In that respect, the monopolistic price policy has a more damaging influence on employment than the monopolistic wage policy.

These brief remarks will, I hope, suffice to demonstrate that those parts of the theory of unemployment that can be explained in a static theory, based, for instance, on the assumption of a constant aggregate demand in terms of money, should be woven into an analysis of the processes of expansion and contraction of total demand. If this is done it will be found that the process of expansion from a depression will usually meet bottlenecks of different sorts long before full employment is reached. A great many problems of adaptation and balancing will have to be met to create the status of full employment. This cannot be done simply by increasing the amount of investment and the aggregate of purchases high enough. To the extent that the Keynesian theory has created the opposite impression, it stands in need of amplification.

I have, after some hesitation, called this chapter "The Swedish Theory of Unused Resources." In a way this is not a very appropriate title, for what has been briefly indicated here is nothing more than a possible combination of the relevant parts of the old static theory of unemployment (which used to be based on some kind of monetary stability assumption) with a theory of processes of monetary expansion and contraction (which is simply an amplification of ordinary business cycle theory). There is, as I have already mentioned, no striking difference between the practical conclusions drawn from this combined theory, which was published in various Swedish books in the years 1933 to 1935, and the general ideas which economists used to believe in, in the 1920s, except that one had become more clearly aware of the fact that an increased disposition to save would not necessarily lead to larger investment. Thus, with regard to conclusions about economic policy, Swedish theory is more conservative than the Keynesian theory, while it claims to cover about the same field and, indeed, to be less dependent on certain special assumptions. Hence it may perhaps be illuminating to attempt, in the next chapter, a comparison between these two theoretical structures and a consideration of some of their practical consequences.

# 7. The Keynesian Theory of Underemployment and Its Practical Application

MANY YEARS AGO in a discussion in Denmark in which I took part, I criticized Karl Marx and "Marxian" economics. One of the people on the other side commented, "Well, of course, every young economist who wants to be a professor must criticize Karl Marx." With more justification it may be said today that it is fashionable to criticize John Maynard Keynes and his theory. That, of course, is a great compliment to the Keynesian economics. I personally hold the opinion that the compliment is well justified. No work in economic theory in the last decades has played anything like so great a role, nor has any deserved it. For, irrespective of which parts of the Keynesian theory will prove to be lasting contributions to economic science, it has stimulated economic thinking in an extraordinary way. Keynes's concepts "propensity to consume" and "liquidity preference"—and his emphasis on formerly insufficiently observed facts and relations in connection with these concepts—have led to a very important addition to our knowledge. I want to emphasize this first because I am going to present some rather critical remarks about certain central aspects of the Keynesian theory and also about the way in which conclusions have been drawn as to practical policy from this simplified theory, based on somewhat unrealistic assumptions about what the economic world is like.

The Keynesian theory is so well known that any summary

of it here would be superfluous. I shall, however, by way of introduction mention nine points in this theory, the nine points which seem to me to make up its most essential parts.

First: Keynes assumes that when the national income rises, the volume of savings will tend to grow and probably more than in proportion to the increase in aggregate incomes. In other words, the marginal propensity to consume declines as incomes go up. People decide to save a larger proportion of their income as incomes rise.

Second: The volume of investment must be large enough to create a market for the part of the total output which is not purchased for consumption—given a certain propensity to consume—because if it were not purchased for investment, then it would not be purchased at all.

Third: Therefore, the volume of output and employment depends on the volume of investment, given a certain propensity to consume. If investment falls below the level that corresponds to the volume of savings in a state of full employment, then the aggregate income will fall until the smaller proportion saved out of a smaller income is just equal to the volume of investment.

Fourth: The inducement to invest depends on the relation between the marginal efficiency of capital and the complex of interest rates. By the marginal efficiency of capital is meant the rate of discount which makes the present value of all future returns of a capital asset equal to the supply price of that asset. It is obvious, says Keynes, that the actual rate of current investment will be pushed to the point where there is no longer any class of capital asset of which the marginal efficiency exceeds the current rate of interest. In other words, Keynes maintains that the expected profit rate at the margin is equal to the rate of interest.

Fifth: The real wage is equal to the marginal productivity of labor in the wage goods industries. The money wage, but not the real wage, depends on the bargaining of workers and employers. Such bargaining can have no influence on the average real wage level, for real wages are entirely determined by the volume of employment, given certain productivity conditions.

Sixth: The marginal productivity of labor falls when employment is expanded.

Seventh: The supply of labor depends on the marginal disutility of labor—an orthodox, classical remnant built into the Keynesian theory, like some others.

Eighth: The rate of interest is determined by the marginal liquidity preference. The rate of interest on a loan of given quality and maturity must be established at the level which equalizes the attractions of holding idle cash and of holding the loan. In other words, the rate of interest equates the supply and demand of idle balances.

Ninth: When a country is growing in wealth somewhat rapidly—measured by western European standards—there is likely to be an insufficiency of the inducements to new investment. In other words, the more or less normal state is one of underinvestment or oversaving, and therefore incomplete employment.

The main part of Keynes's theory can be put in the following equations. (r is the rate of interest, X the investment by public authorities, V the income velocity of money, M the quantity of money, C consumption, E income, S savings and T investment):

$$E\left(1 - \frac{C}{E}\right) = S; \; C = f_1(E); \; S = T; \; T = f_2(r) + X; \; r = f_3\left(M - \frac{E}{V}\right).$$

The form of function $f_1$ depends on the propensity to consume; similarly $f_2$ depends on the marginal productivity of capital and $f_3$ on the liquidity preference.

I turn now to some observations on this theory. I shall try to demonstrate that while it is important and interesting, it is also a highly *special* theory and not at all a *general* theory. I cannot, of course, discuss all the particular assumptions made. Let me mention only in passing that the assumption that savings rise faster than incomes is not essential to the theory. It makes it unnecessarily a special theory. If savings had a tendency to rise in a smaller proportion than income, the theory would nevertheless, on the whole, be the same, although the changes in employment caused by changes in investment would be relatively much larger than in a world where the Keynesian assumption holds good, as I think it does in our society.

Many similarities exist between this theory and the ordinary business cycle theory and the theory worked out in the early thirties as part of an analysis of remedies for unemployment in Sweden. The emphasis in the Keynesian theory is on investment—on changes in the volume of investment. But that, I maintain, has been the case with business cycle theory for at least forty years, and in Knut Wicksell's monetary theory since 1898. It has also, I think, on the whole, been recognized that if you increase the aggregate demand *in a state of unused resources,* you will get an increased output. Therefore, if we increase investment, real income will rise and this will lead to larger consumption. Investment and consumption are not alternatives, if one can increase total output. Should consumption be increased as a result of a decision to save less, an increase in investment may result, because total output goes up. The increase in aggregate income more than offsets the effect on savings of the reduced willingness to save.

I do not think that this part of Keynesian theory regarded as a business cycle theory is novel or revolutionary at all. It is only when it is regarded as part of the orthodox price and distribution theory that one can say: "Isn't this strange, that a nation can decide to save less and yet get a larger volume of investment?"

Let us consider the basic Keynesian equations:

$$E\left(1-\frac{C}{E}\right)=S=T$$

If $\frac{C}{E}$ is the *average* propensity to consume, then $\left(1-\frac{C}{E}\right)$ is the average propensity to save. If we multiply E, which is income, with this propensity to save, then we get the volume of savings, which is equal to investment.

This is the starting point for Keynes's equilibrium theory of employment. An equation of this sort cannot, of course, explain the process of change when investment is varied. The Keynesian reasoning runs in the following way: If investment is reduced, say, by 10 percent, and if $\frac{C}{E}$ is unchanged, income would fall by 10 percent also. However $\frac{C}{E}$ will, of course, vary to some extent. How will it change? One can draw a curve FG for the *marginal* propensity to consume and, thus, for the *marginal* propensity to save. When income declines, the *average* propensity to consume will rise in accordance with the average height of that curve over the base line, and the average propensity to save will decline. The accompanying figure illustrates these relations.

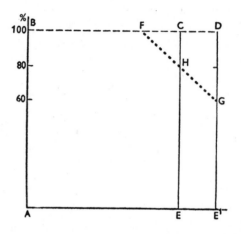

ABCE is the volume of income in position I. FHG is the curve of the marginal propensity to consume. HE as a percentage of CE is 80 percent which is the marginal propensity to consume in position I. When income is increased to ABCE', the marginal propensity to consume falls to 60 percent (GE':DE'). In this position II, the marginal propensity to

save is $\frac{DG}{DE}$. The *average* propensity to save is then $\frac{DGF}{ABDE}$,

The average propensity to save in position II may be, say 12 percent. If investment falls and if the income should go down to position I, then the average propensity to save will be, say 8 percent.

This Keynesian picture of what happens is, I think, much too simplified, for if investment is reduced in a state of relative stability, then the result of production will fall short of expectations. The actual savings will be smaller than the planned savings; there will be an unintentional reduction of savings. Unemployed will draw on their capital and live on credit to some extent. There will also be losses by businessmen, and losses are negative savings items. The savings which are equal to investment are the *ex post* savings, the total volume of savings which have actually been made during a certain period and not the savings illustrated by the curve, which has to do with propensities, that is, savings *plans*.

This is one of the numerous examples where the Keynesian theory fails to distinguish between *"ex post"* and *"ex ante."* The *realized* savings ratio will be smaller than the *planned* savings ratio (which is equal to the average *propensity* to save). It may be that the realized savings ratio will fall from 12 to 8 percent, while the planned ratio will have fallen only to ten. This means that when investment is reduced by a certain percentage the volume of income will not fall so much as the Keynesian theory assumes, because the realized savings will be a smaller proportion of income than this theory assumes. Income will be greater relative to realized savings than before, which means that the income will be greater relative to investment than before, and more so than the Keynesian reasoning explains.

Evidently the volume of realized savings that equals realized investment is not governed only by the volume of income and the propensity to save. It is affected by the whole process that is set in motion and which causes unintentional negative savings, unintentional losses, and so on.

In other words, this equation $E\left(1-\frac{C}{E}\right)=T$ is correct as an *ex post* description, when you look back upon a period. But then it is really only a truism. It follows directly from the definitions of income. If, on the other hand, E, C, and T are *ex ante* concepts concerned with plans (and otherwise the reasoning does not explain anything), the equation does not hold good. It is wrong! It is true that it is not very misleading. It is misleading to the extent that I have explained. Otherwise, the conclusions reached would be much further from reality than they are.[1]

An explanation of a series of events caused by a primary change must run in terms of actions, in terms of plans and expectations, that is, *ex ante* terms. It is necessary to study the relations between the plans and the actions, the ensuing results and their influence on the new plans. This can only be done in a period analysis. It is obvious that as long as plans and realizations differ, we cannot have a stable situation. But neither will this always be the case when the sum total of income that was expected for a certain period agrees with the sum total of income actually earned and when similar investment and savings agree *ex post* and *ex ante*. It is not true, therefore, that such a coincidence indicates an equilibrium in

---

[1] It is, of course a radical simplification to assume that savings by corporations and insurance institutions can be fitted into Keynes's propensity-to-save reasoning, which is based on the behavior of individual consumers. The changes in the decisions to save must be explained in terms of the business policy of corporations with due regard to tax laws, business practices, and so on.

the sense that it is a situation which tends to remain! The agreement with regard to the total categories (planned savings equal realized savings, planned investment equals realized investment, and so on) may hide differences for individuals and for firms. One firm may have better results than expected; another one may have worse. Therefore, in the coming period, plans may differ from the realizations of the earlier period. A relatively low volume of employment in a depression will mean that profits are low for many firms. If this goes on for a certain number of periods, these firms will not continue to act in the same way as hitherto; hence a state of very low profits or losses is not likely to remain fixed. There is no real "equilibrium" in a situation of low volume of investment. It is doubtful if one can profitably call *any* situation an equilibrium situation in the sense that it tends to remain.

To some adherents of the Keynesian school, the volume of investment is regarded as being, on the whole, independent of the disposition to consume and to save. (See Joan Robinson, *Introduction to the Theory of Employment,* London, 1937.) The volume of investment is supposed to vary independently of the other factors. This, however, is an unjustified assumption. Consider a case where people plan to increase investment while the disposition to save is unchanged. What will happen? The volume of investment will rise; but the process which is set in motion will not necessarily increase the volume of savings to the extent of coinciding with the sum of the planned net increase to investments. There may well be *unintentional* reductions in other forms of investment, for instance, in commodity stocks. If people desire to build more than before, it is unlikely that their urge will have been anticipated by the producers of building materials. Stocks of building materials will be reduced. Therefore, the total volume of new investment, if we add together the positive and the negative items, will in many cases be smaller than the sum of the new investments people decided to make. There is a negative item in the unintentional reduction of commodity stocks. The volume of realized savings does not adapt itself completely to the sum of investments decided upon. The realized investment which is equal to realized savings can differ considerably from the planned investment. If there had been other decisions to save more at the same time as the decisions to invest more were made, then the net volume of investment could have reached the planned figure. Stocks of consumers' goods would have risen, thus balancing the fall in other inventories.

Another reason why the static reasoning of the Keynesian theory is unsatisfactory is the fact—well known to Keynes and some of his followers—that the propensity to consume varies with the length of time income has remained fixed. Assume that retailers have *recently* received higher earnings. They may not be certain that this state of affairs is going to last and may not at once base their consumption on the expectation of the same amount of income in all the coming years. To begin with, they play safe, increasing their consumption less than they might have done if they were reasonably certain that the higher income would be permanent. However, when it has remained at the high level for two or three years, it is regarded as "normal" and consumption tends to rise. In other words, the disposition to save and the propensity to consume cannot be explained in static terms. They are dependent on the *development* of income, because this development affects expectations concerning income and plans to buy and to save.

It is impossible to maintain that the expectation of income for a future period depends only on what was earned in the last period, particularly if the length of that period is not stipulated. Obviously the expectation is often dependent on the incomes earned during *a series* of earlier periods, even if we consider periods as long as a calendar year, and on many other circumstances as well.

What I have said above seems to me to warrant the conclusion that the Keynesian idea of a stable equilibrium of underemployment, governed by the volume of investment and a certain propensity to consume in the simple way the equation indicates, cannot be maintained. The explanation of the relation between changes in investment and changes in income has to be an analysis of a time-using process where the distinction between plans and actual results is essential.

### THE MULTIPLIER

Let me come now to some observations on *the multiplier theory,* which is only, so to speak, the reverse side of the Keynesian equation above.

The *marginal* multiplier is the relation between the increment of *income* and the increment of *investment.* It varies with changes in the national income; it declines when incomes go up, for example as a result of improved business conditions; for the marginal propensity to save rises when income is increased—if the consumption function is constant. Thus, the income created by the new investment will lead to new demand for consumption purposes to a lesser extent when employment is high, than when it is low. But the marginal multiplier will change in the course of a business cycle for two other reasons, of which the first is entirely ignored and the second not sufficiently observed by the Keynesian school. The first reason is the fact that actual savings differ from planned savings, as we have seen. The marginal realized savings ratio varies much more than the marginal planned savings ratio, because there are unexpected losses in a depression and unexpected gains in a boom. Unintentional changes in savings are negative when the national income falls, and they are positive when the national income goes up. And this makes the marginal realized savings ratio and the marginal multiplier vary to a much greater degree than is obvious from a study of the disposition to save and invest, only.

Furthermore, as already mentioned, the consumption function is probably not so constant as some adherents of the Keynesian theory assume.[2] It varies with the whole economic situation—with the length of the period of time a group of people have enjoyed an increased income. There is in the multiplier theory a tendency to pay relatively little attention to *time* in another sense also. All the indirect reactions—of 1) consumption, 2) secondary employment, 3) secondary increases in consumption, 4) investment—are part of a time-using process. If one is to sum up this declining series of increments of purchases into a sum that expresses the total increase

---

[2]Keynes himself is noncommittal on this point. The practical value in an analysis of policy in concrete cases of the multiplier concept is, of course, much dependent on whether the propensity to consume is relatively stable or fairly so, and if its behavior during booms and depressions follows a regular pattern that can be ascertained in advance. This, however, seems very doubtful.

in income when investment is increased by a certain amount, one has to ask how long a time it takes before all these indirect reactions have appeared. There may be months between number two and number three, and there may be half a year between parts of number three and number four. It may be that long before all the reactions have appeared, the whole situation has changed and you have new tendencies that make the others irrelevant for economic policy.

The fact that little attention is paid to the time element is of course not due to chance, or because economists haven't happened to think about it. It is because the Keynesian theory is a static *equilibrium* theory; if it had been a dynamic theory, that is, an analysis of a time-using process, it would have been absolutely impossible not to study the length of the period of time which the reactions require, and the effects of the probable or possible changes in the propensity to consume that are called forth in the process set in motion by the original change in investment.

The main reason, however, why I think that the multiplier theory is not one of the useful parts of the Keynesian theory is not what I have said above, but the fact that it really studies only half the picture and an arbitrary part of what happens. If we are interested in the consequences of a certain increase in the volume of investment—for example the effects of certain public works—we do not want to know only how much more *consumers* will buy. We must know also how the profit expectations and *investment purchases* will be affected. When sales begin to expand, businessmen will become less pessimistic and will increase their investment. This reaction of investment may be just as important as the reaction of consumers' purchases.

The total influence on production and income of an increase
in public works depends on the reactions both of the consumers
and of the professional buyers, the investors. Furthermore, the
expansion of private investment influences the volume of consumption. Of course once we introduce the investment purchases into the picture, it is obvious that these are very capricious and dependent on the circumstances in each case. A
certain public investment, say five billion dollars, in one situation will bring about almost no reaction from private investment, because businessmen are afraid, many of them perhaps
considering it an "unsound" policy, as happened in 1933
and 1934 in the United States. At another time an increase
in public investment by five billion dollars may raise private
investment by ten billion dollars or more after a couple of
years.

For this reason—and the others I have mentioned above—
it is quite possible that if we consider the whole increase in
income that is caused by a certain increase in investment, it
may be ten times larger than the original increase in investment in one period. In another situation it may not be larger
at all. The numerous econometric attempts to compute the
size of what should be called "the consumption multiplier"
seem to me to be rather uninteresting, even misleading, chiefly
because they leave out of account the secondary reactions of
investment purchases and their effects on consumption.

KEYNES'S WAGE THEORY

As I mentioned by way of introduction, in this theory real
wages are equal to the marginal productivity of labor in the
wage goods industries. Hence, increased employment will al-

ways mean lower real wages, given certain productivity conditions.[3] This is, of course, entirely orthodox, classical doctrine. The real wages depend only on the volume of employment, and the poor trade unions cannot raise them, unless they create unemployment. But this again must be an oversimplification. First of all, we have been taught by the imperfect competition theory that marginal costs do not tend to be equal with the value of the marginal product. It is not true that you can take the value of the marginal product of labor and assume that wages tend to coincide with this value. Marginal costs tend to be equal to marginal *revenue,*[4] and marginal revenue is not the same as the value of the marginal product, except in industries where perfect competition reigns. Marginal revenue, as everyone knows, is equal to the value of the marginal product, *minus* what a firm "loses" when it reduces price for the "earlier product" in order to sell more.

This fact alone invalidates the classical and Keynesian reasoning about real wages. It can be put this way: When business conditions improve as a result of increased foreign purchases or larger public works, an increase in the aggregate demand in terms of money may increase employment without reducing the real wage; for at constant prices, the marginal revenue—and, thus, nominal and real wages—need not fall. They can even rise.

[3]In a paper on "Relative Movements of Real Wages and Output," *The Economic Journal,* 1939, Keynes admits some possible inadequacies of this theory. My discussion below deals with some other aspects.

[4]It is another story to what extent businessmen are actually led by a marginal reasoning. In my opinion their reasons for moving price above or reducing it below "normal capacity average total costs," including "fair" profits, can often be better described in other terms. But it would carry me too far to analyze this question here.

Let us take the case of a firm selling at a constant price—as many firms do. When production is increased, marginal *production* costs tend to go up, if nominal wage rates are constant. It pays the firm to spend money on sales promotion until a point is reached when marginal *selling* costs—the cost of selling one unit more at a constant price—are considered equal to the difference between price and marginal production costs (see the accompanying chart).

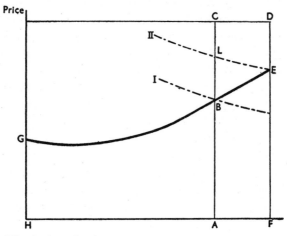

GBE=Marginal production costs curve

  BC=Marginal selling costs when HA is produced and sold in situation I

  CL=Marginal selling costs when HA is produced and sold in situation II

  AB=Marginal production costs when HA is produced and sold

If the aggregate demand is increased—the demand curve being shifted to the right—it will be easy to sell more goods, with no more advertising, and even with less. The influence of the increase in aggregate demand will be that marginal selling costs fall from BC to CL, if HA units are to be sold. They will be ED when HF units of goods are put on the market. If prices are maintained, the HF quantity will be sold, marginal production costs will be EF and marginal selling costs DE. It is quite conceivable, therefore, that an increase in the total purchasing power and demand will bring about an expansion of sales from A to F. Nominal wage rates, prices, and real wages may remain unchanged.

Let us consider a case of this kind, in which the marginal production cost curve is raised as a result of nominal wage increases. It may nevertheless be profitable to sell at unchanged prices a greater volume of goods than in the original situation, although probably a smaller quantity than would have been sold if wage rates had not risen. An increase in employment need not increase profits through a decline in wages. Both wages and profits may rise.

I have often met businessmen who have said, "Why, of course, if I can expand my sales in a growing market, I can pay a higher wage and yet sell at the same price." If you say it does not agree with the marginal price theory—as I used to say in the 1920s—the businessmen are apt to answer, "Well, I don't know, but it is a fact nevertheless. I do know that I pay higher wages and I do sell at the same price, and it pays me to do so."

It is interesting to observe that the influence of a change in the total volume of aggregate demand under conditions of imperfect competition has been neglected in the Keynesian theory. In other connections, this theory emphasizes the effects of a change in the national income and thus in the aggregate demand, but it ignores its effect on "sales resistance."

A more realistic theory of the demand for labor as well as for other productive factors, must, I think, first analyze why firms decide to expand or restrict output; the analysis should be primarily, though not exclusively, in marginal revenue terms. To this must be added an analysis of the combination of the productive factors—their relative proportions—in marginal productivity terms. In this way, the demand both for labor and raw material can be explained. It is a joint demand, which the orthodox marginal productivity theory of wages fails to consider. Of course, the demand for productive factors to expand output depends on expectations; for example, the expected marginal revenue, which need not be equal to the present marginal revenue. These deviations of the expected from the present revenue may be important. In analyzing investment, that is, the demand for capital goods, Keynes pays a good deal of attention to expectations. To a considerable extent should not the same reasoning be applicable with regard to the demand for labor?

One reason why, I think, trade unions have a considerable scope for their activities and power to influence average real wage rates in manufacturing industries is that the marginal selling costs are very difficult to estimate. I have often asked businessmen about the marginal selling costs—how they measure the effect of advertising upon sales. We all know the new technique for measuring this effect; but in spite of the progress thereby attained the conclusion is inescapable that businessmen know very little about *marginal* selling costs and how to measure them. They seem to rely upon intuition, or something very like it.[5]

If trade unions force up wage rates—thereby raising marginal production costs—it need not have any immediate influence on the price policy of the firms. It may and it may not. This margin of uncertainty gives the trade unions a greater chance of influencing real wage rates without bringing about a drop in employment. The rise in wages will be at the expense largely of the business profits, although aggregate selling costs may decline.

It would be a rather important practical conclusion—if the Keynesian theory were correct—that trade unions cannot influence the real wage level but can only influence the relative wage levels for different kinds of labor. If so, we could save a lot of effort in labor organizations. It is, on the other hand, a serious deficiency of the Keynesian theory, if it should be wrong, as I think it is, on this point as well as with regard to the relation between real wages and employment. It ignores both the changes in marginal selling costs, when the market situation varies under the influence of variations in the national income and aggregate demand, and the indeterminateness of these costs, and does not pay sufficient attention to expectations.

KEYNES'S INTEREST THEORY

To Keynes, the rate of interest has to equalize the attractions of holding cash and of holding a loan. It is a simple

---

[5] A similar reasoning is applicable in cases where the firms vary prices. For the marginal revenue is then as difficult to estimate in a concrete situation as the marginal selling costs above.

theory. As a matter of fact, I think that its simplicity is one of its advantages and the reason why it has been so effectively "sold" to the public and the economists. The rate of interest is a function of the quantity of money, after deduction of the quantity of money that is needed for circulation. Under certain conditions as to income and with a certain velocity of money, the market needs for circulation a certain quantity of money; what remains is that quantity of money which can be called "idle balances." The rate of interest is a function of the quantity of idle balances. It must equalize the demand for and supply of idle balances, which are determined by "external" forces. Demand depends on the income earned by different people and also on the rate of interest.

Keynes's rate of interest is a differential rate—what must be paid to make people abstain from wanting to keep more money idle than is available. When money is idle, it yields no return, the theory assumes. But in many countries, for instance in Sweden before the war, interest was paid on checking accounts. The Keynesian theory does not fit this case. Compare the Ricardian theory of land rent, which assumed that there is always some kind of land that gives no rent.

Of course, it may be said that the existing rate of interest—or rates of interest—must be such as to make people willing to hold the existing amount of cash or idle balances, but it must also make them willing to hold the total available quantity of different kinds of loans and the total available quantity of shares. Thus, supply must equal demand for all these assets at the existing rates of interest. The rates of interest are influenced by the fact that someone must hold not only the idle balances, but the loans, the shares, and so on. This would seem to be a more general approach than the Keynesian one, but not fundamentally different. The rates of interest are governed by the supply and demand for different kinds of credit and for cash. Strangely enough the Keynesian school does not agree to this, as far as I know. To Keynes, the rate of interest is either determined entirely from the outside—his special theory—or is dependent only on the quantity of idle balances, given a certain distribution of income and a certain liquidity preference.

One advantage of the approach I have suggested in the preceding chapter is that attention is directed to the connection between changes in output, income and savings, on the one hand, and changes in the willingness and ability to make financial investment, to buy bonds and buy shares, and so on, on the other. There is a connection between changes in different parts of the economic system, changes in interest rates and changes in the willingness to hold different assets. It is highly important that this connection is not overlooked.

According to Keynes, there is "for every rate of interest, a certain volume of employment for which this rate of interest is the natural rate, in the sense that the system will be in equilibrium with that rate of interest and that level of employment."[6] Now this, I think, is a static reasoning. It is more realistic to say that, for each possible economic development in a country, there is a rate of interest or a complex of interest rates compatible with that economic development. Of course, in some cases several rates of interest may be compatible with the assumed development. In other cases there is none. This is not very far from the Keynesian idea, except that his statement runs in terms of a situation, while my own is in terms of a development.

[6] See the discussion in the *Economic Journal*, September, 1937, p. 242.

Keynes made the following illuminating statement about his theory: "The initial novelty lies in my maintaining that it is not the rate of interest but the level of incomes which insure equality between savings and investment."[7] The rate of interest does affect investment and income and, thereby, savings. It does not directly affect savings, in any case, the direct influence is small compared with the indirect one that goes *via* changes in income. In the last chapter of *General Theory* on "Social Implications," he indicates that savings are to some extent directly affected by the height of the rate of interest.

The neutral, or optimum, rate of interest, Keynes says, is that rate which is "consistent with full employment, given the other parameters of the system" (*General Theory*, p. 243). Now, it is of course not at all certain that such a rate exists in all situations. If it did, we would only have to have the correct interest policy to insure permanent full employment. (Compare the more dynamic analysis I have presented in the preceding chapter.)

Let me add only a few words to characterize the Keynesian doctrine of *investment* and of *labor supply*. It is asserted that the volume of investment is carried up to the point where the expected marginal profit rate is equal to the rate of interest. This seems to me to be a highly simplified description, usable only as a first introduction. For many years I have been questioning businessmen about their attitude toward new investment. The conversation often runs like this: "How much new investment have you planned?" "We have plans worked out more or less in detail for profitable new investment amounting to about five million dollars." "How much are you carrying

[7] *Ibid.*, p. 250.

out now?" "Investments for two million dollars." *"Why not more?"* That is the crucial question. I have received many different answers. In some cases, they do not want to borrow money to finance the new investment. In other cases, they do not think it advisable to disturb production by too sudden changes, and so on. One thing seems certain. The behavior of businessmen is not well described by saying that they try to realize all those investments immediately that promise a net return equal to or above the relevant rate of interest. A more refined analysis in terms of risks and chances is called for. A pioneer piece of research in this field has been done by some Oxford economists. It should, I think, be continued.

Keynes's labor supply theory is that the supply of labor is determined by the marginal disutility of work and the marginal utility of the wage. This is no doubt a very orthodox and special theory. In many countries working hours are limited to forty or forty-eight hours. If people are to work more, they will require overtime pay—50 or 100 percent additional pay. Only a certain amount of overtime is allowed. The supply of labor under such conditions cannot be adequately analyzed in terms of the marginal disutility of labor: a more "institutional" description is, I think, necessary.

### THE TENDENCY TO OVERSAVING

It falls outside the scope of my analysis to demonstrate that Keynes—in a work called *General Theory of Employment*—pays relatively little attention to those kinds of unemployment, often called "structural," which are called forth by entirely different circumstances than an insufficient volume of investment. Such unemployment may be due to monopolistic price policies, price and wage maladjustments, insufficient mobility of labor, and so on. In the 1920s Great Britain offered important examples of such phenomena.[8] Instead of commenting upon this matter, I shall add a few words about some practical applications of Keynes's theory with special reference to those parts of economic policy which may have an influence on savings. Keynes bases his recommendations on the assumption that there is in western European capitalist society a tendency to oversaving that endangers full employment. Investment as a rule falls short of the savings of a full employment situation. Hence, taxation and other measures so constructed as to reduce savings may be highly beneficial. "Ancient Egypt was doubly fortunate—and doubtless owes to this its fabled wealth—in that it possessed two activities, namely, pyramid building as well as the search for precious metals, the fruits of which, since they could not serve the needs of Man by being consumed, did not stale with abundance. The Middle Ages built cathedrals and sang dirges, etc."[9]

Evidently Keynes assumes that even in Egypt and in Europe in the Middle Ages there was a tendency to oversaving. It is only because the Egyptians were fortunate enough to get this brilliant idea of building pyramids that they were saved

[8]The relatively scanty attention that has been given by the Keynesians to structural unemployment and the existence of various bottlenecks has sometimes led to a belief that almost all unemployment can be cured by expansionary measures—an increase in total investment or total consumption. In my opinion, an analysis in terms of changes in such total categories is relatively satisfactory in a state of serious depression, when surplus capacity exists everywhere in industry, but it is in need of much amplification when employment is on a somewhat higher level, even though far from a full employment level. For a brief discussion of structural unemployment see the end of last chapter.

[9]*General Theory*, p. 131.

from mass unemployment and could create their "fabulous wealth." In other words, economically useless investment, even under those conditions, increased wealth! It has often been asserted that British economics is a generalization of British experience during the lifetime of the respective British economists. While I am a great admirer of British economics, I do not think that this criticism is entirely without foundation. But I think Keynes has established a record in generalizing the experience of Great Britain and the United States in the 1930s and in applying it to ancient Egypt and the Middle Ages.

Keynes did not, of course, mean us to interpret his historical parallels too literally. Yet, one has to ask whether there were not other reasons, than the one he advanced, for unemployment in the earlier centuries, if we may speak of unemployment in the modern sense during economic conditions so widely different from ours. One may also ask whether the fabled wealth in Egypt was not an outstanding example of a very uneven distribution of income, of riches among mass poverty.

It is a much more serious question whether Keynes's view about modern conditions in our type of society is correct. Frankly, I do not think that it is. One of his arguments runs like this: "Experience suggests that in existing conditions savings by institutions and through sinking funds is more than adequate and that measures which discourage savings may prove positively favorable to the growth of capital."[10]

But, why should outlets for new investments be insufficient? It is true that there have been booms with incomplete employment in spite of the optimism that rules in business during such periods. But this may be due to the fact that the volume of

[10]*Ibid.*, p. 373.

investment in the preceding depression was very low and that, as a consequence, it could not be rapidly expanded without meeting bottlenecks that caused a considerable rise in costs; for example, the supply of new building labor may have been small in the depression and the rise in wage rates rapid when business and building activity recovered. It is not improbable that one of the worst risks to the maintenance of a high level of employment in the United States in the coming years is the limited supply and the age composition of building labor. A relative rise in building costs may convince many potential buyers of new houses that they had better wait and see. Such a "maladjustment" is, of course, no evidence of a permanent tendency to "oversaving." It can be cured by an adaptation of labor supply and costs in the investment trades.

It is strange indeed that in the discussion of the oversaving question by the Keynesian school so little attention has been paid to the height of the interest level. Would not the demand for housing space grow enormously, if the rate of interest were zero, that is, if money could be borrowed at a rate that covers only risk and handling charges? A fall in the interest rate would also, I think, tend to reduce savings. This Keynes denies in the main parts of *General Theory*. However, on second thought, in the last chapter on social implications, Keynes becomes uncertain. He writes as follows: "It may turn out that the propensity to consume will be so easily strengthened by the effects of a fall in the rate of interest, that full employment can be reached with a rate of accumulation that is only a little greater than at present. I must not be supposed to deny the possibility or even the probability of this outcome."[11]

[11]*General Theory*, p. 377.

I entirely agree with this sentence. We do not know to what extent a drop in the interest level would lead to an expansion of investment and a fall in savings. But, its influence in these directions would probably be considerable. The fact that employment is sensitive to changes in investment at home and abroad and the fact that private investment is likely to vary is an argument, first of all, for a relatively low rate of interest in a state of underemployment and a high rate in booms, unless other methods to discourage investment are used. It is also an argument for a determined public policy to vary public investment in a useful way, and thirdly an argument for economic flexibility, including measures against monopolistic wage and trading policies, particularly in the investment industries. But, it is no valid reason for measures to reduce permanently the willingness of people to save.[12]

I do not think that there is a sufficient foundation even for the conclusion that it would be much easier to maintain full employment if the propensity to save were permanently low— and thus the savings relatively small—than if it were higher, within the limits of experience in capitalist countries. It is possible that the combination of low interest rates and a determined government policy of "stabilization" would be able to keep up the aggregate quantity of investment and employment and thus prevent large setbacks, at least if international collaboration can be guaranteed. It is, of course, also possible that

---

[12]According to the National City Bank report (Nov. 1947) estimates of the Securities and Exchange Commission indicate that in the United States individuals in all added nothing net during 1946 to their holdings of corporate stocks and bonds. Individual savings took the form of institutionalized savings, reflected in accumulation of insurance and pension funds, or savings in anticipation of consumption.

such a policy will fail—it will depend largely on the political conditions—but so far we have not made any serious attempt to carry it out. Our experience, therefore, is inconclusive, and it was much too early in the 1930s to recommend a policy of reduced savings, particularly at a time when countries with another economic system (I am thinking particularly of Russia) maintained a very high savings ratio. The destruction of World War II has in most countries made only too obvious what was true even before the war: that a policy to maintain confidence in the monetary system and to encourage savings is much more called for than a weakening of the propensity to save. This, however, is a value judgment from which everybody is free to differ, even while accepting my view that the possibility of maintaining a high level of employment in a free-enterprise economy is not much smaller in a society with a large average savings ratio than in a society where consumption is relatively high.

In the beginning of this chapter I have emphasized the fact that the contributions to our knowledge about the economic world that have been made by Keynes in his *General Theory* are very important, for example, his discussion of liquidity preference and the marginal propensity to consume. He also combines pieces of old knowledge in a new and illuminating way. This is particularly true of his use of the relation between changes in investment and in total production and income. However, his theoretical method is that of a static equilibrium theory, which is easy to teach to students but from the point of view of method is a step backwards. It has led Keynes and others into such serious errors as the neglect of important aspects of the connection between savings and investment. As indicated above, a more realistic theory has to run in terms of a time-using process.

The "revolutionary" flavor of the Keynesian theory is chiefly due to its application to cases where special assumptions are made (for example, concerning a quasi-permanent tendency to oversaving) and also to the fact that these cases are regarded as characteristic of our society. If the practical conclusions concerning policy are regarded as valid in a depression economy only, they do not differ much from the earlier teachings about business cycles. There has certainly been no revolution in economic science in the 1930s and it is important that students of our science should not be led into a false belief in such a revolution. As a matter of fact, it is more natural to stress the continuity of the scientific development than the reverse.

# Appendix

Experience seems to demonstrate that strict price control often fails to keep down profits. Part of the explanation of this surprising fact may be the following.

Assume a situation of relatively high employment. Fig. 1 illustrates the case of a "typical" commodity produced by a certain firm in imperfect competition.

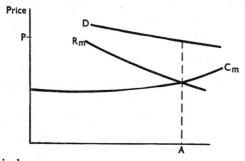

Cm=Marginal cost
Rm=Marginal revenue
 D=Demand curve

Price control is introduced, price stop is declared at the level P.

Assume that the aggregate demand rises owing to an increase in investment activity in the country as a whole without any increase in the propensity to save. The demand curve for the commodity *a* is shifted to the right. Owing to government price control prices cannot be raised. Output with existing capacity and labor force can only be expanded to OB, but OC can be sold at the existing price. BC is unsatisfied demand. The dotted line PF + FG is the demand curve for commodity *a* from the point

of view of this firm. As long as output and sales fall short of OC
price is equal to marginal revenue and exceeds marginal costs. If
there were no price control, the price would be raised and, assuming that this did not enable the firm to draw more labor

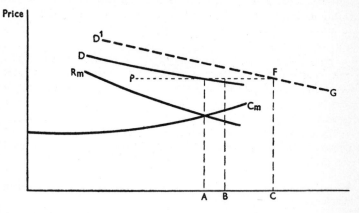

from other occupations, a quantity OB of this commodity or a
little less, depending on the slope of the new marginal revenue
curve (not drawn on the diagram), would be sold.

   If the available capacity of the industrial plant and of other
means of production is relatively low compared to the number of
workers seeking employment, then the marginal cost of output in
a situation of over-full employment will be considerably higher
than in a case of 10 or 20 percent less employment. The prices
that can be fixed by the price control must cover marginal costs
in firms with relatively high costs, otherwise output will not be
forthcoming. Hence the difference between total revenue and
total variable costs will be larger than when the marginal cost
curve is more nearly horizontal and when the prices can, therefore, be fixed by the control at a lower level. As a matter of fact,
however, there is an important reason why the prices fixed by the
control should exceed the marginal costs for most products in a

state of over-full employment. For otherwise, it would pay the firms to produce less of goods that barely cover marginal costs and more of other goods that can be produced in the same plant or in the same firm by the same labor force. The price-controlling authorities are as a rule anxious to avoid large dislocations of output, and, hence—unless direct regulation of output is used—have to allow prices above marginal costs, even if such prices should give relatively large profits in many lines.

If, on the other hand, marginal cost curves are flat in the relevant intervals, i.e., if there is a surplus capacity with regard to plant in a situation where almost all workers are employed, it should prove easier to keep prices on a level that does not give large profits than it will be if marginal cost curves rise steeply.[1]

The fact that marginal revenue exceeds marginal cost is, of course, a stimulus to increase the labor force even if it should require some rise in the wage rates paid by the firm.

[1]See an interesting paper by Alvin H. Hansen, "Cost Functions and Full Employment," *The American Economic Review,* 1947.

# Index